All American Cars and Trucks

A Consumer's Guidebook To The Best

All American Cars and Trucks

Warren Brown

National
Press
Books

Washington, D.C.

Library of Congress Cataloging-in-Publication Data

Brown, Warren, 1948 -
    All American cars & trucks / by Warren Brown.
        192 pp., 18cm by 23cm.
    ISBN 1-882605-05-5 : $11.95
    1. Automobiles — United States — Performance — Testing.
    2. Trucks — United States — Performance — Testing.
    I. Title. II Title: All American cars and trucks.
        TL285.B73 1993
    93-34250 629.28'24'0973 — dc20 CIP

PRINTED IN THE UNITED STATES OF AMERICA
1 2 3 4 5 6 7 8 9 10

Dedication

To Frank Swoboda, who gave me a chance; Mary Anne

Reed-Brown, who gave me the encouragement and time

to pursue that chance; I. Rajeswary, for help beyond the

call of duty; Kathleen Hunter, who taught me how to

drive a stick; and to Anne Veigle, who in 1985 told me

that there is a story behind every car, and that all of

those stories have something to do with love — and sex.

Table of Contents

Chapter 1:
Just a Little Lovin'
Small Cars and Wagons — $8,000-$18,000

Chapter 2:
When Ozzie Met Harriet
Mid-size Family Cars and Wagons — $15,000 to $26,000

Chapter 3

Hot Dates Saturday Night

Affordable Sports Coupes and Convertibles — $13,000 to $23,000

Chapter 4

Livin' Large

Full-size and Luxury American Automobiles

Chapter 5
Too Hot To Handle

Super American Sports Machines — Money's No Object

Chapter 6
Long-Haul Lovin'

Pickup Trucks

Chapter 7

The Brady Bunch

Minivans for the Whole Family

Chapter 8

The Rough-Riders

Four-Wheel Drive Sport Utility Vehicles

Warren's Top Picks

Small Cars and Wagons/$8,000-$18,000

1. Chevrolet Cavalier. Yes, the homely Chevrolet Cavalier.
2. Any Saturn, even with the generator wiring defect that prompted a recall in August 1993.
3. Toyota Corolla/Geo Prizm. Truly nice, make-you-happy subcompacts.
4. Plymouth Sundance, without the Duster foolishness.

Mid-size Family Cars and Wagons/ $15,000 to $26,000

1. Chrysler LH models, as a group, Dodge Intrepid, Chrysler Concorde and Eagle Vision.
2. Ford Taurus/Mercury Sable, combined duo. Ditto above-mentioned reasons.
3. Pontiac Bonneville SSE, sans the SSEi package. Ozzie and Harriet on love pills.
4. Toyota Camry. Just a nice-looking, well-made, but sometimes overpriced thing.

Affordable Sports Coupes and Convertibles, from $13,000 to $23,000

1. Ford Mustang. Hands-down. Light, tight and dyn-O-mite.
2. Pontiac Firebird/Chevrolet Camaro. Truly hot. The essence of tumescence.
3. Ford Probe. Lives up to its name.

Full-size and Luxury American Automobiles

1. Lincoln Mark VIII — A simply beautiful automobile, inside and out.
2. Cadillac Eldorado Touring Coupe — This is Cadillac resurrected!
3. Chrysler New Yorker — It's a damned fine car, period.
4. Buick Park Avenue Ultra — Excellent overall design (I really love this car).
5. Cadillac Seville STS — Someone with taste has finally taken over Cadillac design.

Pickup Trucks

1. GMC Sonoma/Chevy S Series. Totally hip compact trucks. Well-made. Well-designed.
2. Ford Ranger. Always one of my favorites. I just like the way it feels and rides.

Minivans for the Whole Family

1. Plymouth Voyager, Dodge Caravan, Chrysler Town & Country. Hands-down.
2. Nissan Quest/Mercury Villager. Hot on Chrysler's tail.
3. GMC Safari. Love it for different reasons, especially when those reasons involve hauling…

Four-Wheel Drive Sport Utility Vehicles

1. Jeep Grand Cherokee. Expensive. But a damned nice suvvie, especially off-road.
2. Ford Explorer. An excellent all-around suvvie, more for families than for hauling and pulling.

Acknowledgments

Here's praise for the schleppers, the grunts who transport hundreds of new cars and trucks across the country, often sacrificing weekends and holidays, so that folks like me can see 'em, drive 'em, and write about 'em.

Valerie Klabouch, formerly of A&M Specialists Inc., is the queen of test-car schlepping, a job she now does exclusively for BMW of North America. Thanks also to Carol Malkus, Kathy and Dawn Dahlstrom, and John Thompson, all of A&M.

And thanks to Fred Mackerodt Inc.'s proprietors, Fred Mackerodt and Christy Woods Mackerodt, and to their roadmen, Bruno de Vooght and Chet Tomich — and George Taylor, a talented actor who drives between performances.

Thanks to Michael Geylin and Stuart Schorr of Kermish-Geylin Public Relations; to Marty Schorr and the people at Performance Media Public Relations; to Peter Farrell Motor Services; the Prietive Group; and to free-lance vehicle-transport maven Richard Fehr, who also writes books.

High-fives to Ford Motor Co.'s Barbara Mansfield, and to Kathy Lemke Menuet, a former Ford employee who writes splendid children's stories. And special thanks to Jodi Williams and Carol LaCovey, both of General Motors Corp.'s Washington office, and to James Farmer, mouthpiece cum laude for Saturn Corp.

And thanks to Toyota Motor Corp. — yeah, Toyota, the Japanese company that makes American mid-size sedans in Georgetown, Ky., and American subcompact cars and trucks in Fremont, Calif. Thanks to Toyota's Fred Hammond and Lisa Weissman.

To write about cars and trucks, you've got to drive 'em; and to drive 'em, you've got to get 'em. The above-mentioned people and transport organizations got 'em to me on time every time.

And thanks to my banker and full-time employer — the *Washington Post*, which paid many of the bills related to the test vehicles and which provided a healthy circulation base for the "Wheels" column that appears every Friday in the newspaper's *Weekend Magazine*. The column is syndicated nationwide through the Los Angeles Times-Washington Post News Service, for which I am also grateful.

Thanks to former *Washington Post* Business editor Frank Swoboda and former *Weekend* editor Ben Cason for approving the original column idea; to former *Weekend* assignment editors Jeanne Cooper and John Cotter, for getting "Wheels" off to a good start; to current *Weekend* editors Don Brazeal, John Kelly and Roger Piantadosi, for allowing me to write the way I feel; and to chief *Weekend* editorial aide Bruce Walker, who keeps the checks coming on time.

Introduction

I've never regarded cars and trucks as appliances, and never met anyone who does. Not even consumer advocate Ralph Nader. To him, motor vehicles are a cause, an evil to be dealt with, a collective symbol of business run amok. I've disagreed with some of Nader's ideas, sometimes in print. But I've always admired the passion he brought to the job of keeping the auto industry, particularly the American auto industry, rolling straight.

Had it not been for the popularity of cars and trucks, Nader might've been unknown. Most certainly, his landmark book, *Unsafe At Any Speed*, "the book that changed the way America builds its automobiles," would not have been written.

Nader's book hit many people where they live and die — behind the wheel. Look at any major expressway at any time of day, and what you'll see are hundreds of cars and trucks, poet Kathleen Hunter's "prismed stars," speeding "with militant organized urgency."

Lives and dreams are in those vehicles — coming from, or going to someone or something, escaping momentarily, or perhaps engaging in some act of commercial deliverance, legal or otherwise. Most of those lives will ripen with age. Others will not, will instead become part of the annual highway fatality rate — two deaths per 100 million vehicle miles, 43,500 traffic fatalities, including pedestrians felled by motor trips gone awry.

Still, many people love their cars and trucks, and will not part with them, unless forced to do so. Those people include utilitarians who are fond of boasting about the ordinariness of vehicles in their possession.

I understand this passion. It has something to do with freedom. That was made clear to me as a black child growing up in New Orleans, La.

Back then, in the 1950s and early 1960s, I had to step to the rear of public transports, carrying my dignity as best I could. But I could sit in the front seat of my parents' Rambler American, Chevrolet Caprice, or Cadillac Brougham. I'd watch with pride as my father or mother took command of the wheel, in charge of personal destiny, if only for the duration of the trip.

Riding in those cars was my way of hiding out from Jim Crow. But things changed. Riding became driving, and hiding out became making out in the back seats of big American mobiles — *mea culpa, mea culpa, mea maxima culpa*.

There were no foreign cars back then, none that we Louisiana car lovers paid attention to, anyway. Unfortunately, U.S. automakers made the same mistake; and they got their butts kicked in the 1970s and 1980s, losing more than 30 percent of their home market to foreign rivals.

Today, things are turning around and the U.S. auto industry is coming back — but with a difference. "American" cars and trucks now include any vehicle built in the United States, Canada, or Mexico, and sold on U.S. shores.

Traditionalists disagree with that notion. I disagree with the traditionalists. Is a Ford Crown Victoria made in Canada with less than 75-percent U.S. content more "American" than a Mazda 626 made in Flat Rock, Mich., with 75-percent U.S. content? I don't think so. I accept the new definition of "American" metal. Cars such as the Mazda 626 and Ford Crown Vic both get stars and stripes treatment in this book.

There is another definitional conundrum that must be resolved here, thanks to the government's knack for defining identical items several different ways. At issue is the politically inspired confusion over what's a "car" and what's a "truck."

Let me make it simple:
• In this book, a "car" is a coupe, sedan, roadster, or station wagon.
• "Light trucks" include minivans, full-size vans, sport-utility vehicles, and pick-ups. Three U.S. government agencies — the National Highway Traffic Safety Administration, the Environmental Protection Agency, and the Internal Revenue Service — classify "light trucks" that way. One agency, U.S. Customs, does not. This is a democracy. Three to one wins.

This book attempts to segregate cars into size and price groupings, based on their rankings in the vehicle-size classification list compiled by the Automotive News Data Center. Of course, size and price don't necessarily correspond to one another. Thus, there is some overlap, some shading of distinction in the groupings presented here.

Keep in mind that this book is not meant to be a technical tome, no more than the myriad cars and trucks available in the U.S. market are meant to be joyless renditions of mechanical assembly. Important consumer information is provided; but, mostly, this book is a collection of impressions about American vehicles and the world in which they're driven.

It's a book about cars and life and trucks and fun, and gripes — and a little bit of sex.

— Warren Brown

Prelude

Southfield Expressway, 7 a.m.

The onrush of prismed stars
Speed with militant organized urgency
Through the early grays of the November morning
Tires whining in monotone down the slick lanes.
If you will risk smothering the static wails of W-C-A-R
There is a moment of privacy
Between the half finished coffee and toast
and your absolute destiny for the next eight hours —
A moment to ask questions too hard to consider anywhere else.
(Here you know exactly where you have to be right now
and where you're going.)
What it means and why you are doing it

Yesterday?

This morning?

Thirty-and-out?

It's not the answers you need so much as the chance to question
And wonder if it could have been different.

— *Kathleen Hunter*

1

Just a Little Lovin'

Small Cars and Wagons — $8,000 to $18,000

CHEVROLET Cavalier VL

It was back to Detroit, which meant back to humble metal. It's risky to drive anything else in that City of Light Fingers and Quick Hands, where car theft is a growth industry.

I rented a 1993 Chevrolet Cavalier VL (Value Leader), one of many Cavaliers I've used on Detroit trips.

The VL is the least expensive car in the Cavalier line, which has prices ranging from $8,500 to over $18,000, with the top sticker belonging to the Cavalier Z24 convertible. And, hey, there was a Z24 available. But it's kind of nuts to drive a soft-top car in a hard-knock town.

The little VL did just fine, thank you. It zipped up and down Detroit's expressways with competence. It moved through the city's rougher neighborhoods in peace. I parked the car overnight in a guarded garage. But real peace of mind came from knowing that no thief worthy of the name would touch the thing.

Background: The Cavalier entered the U.S. market in 1982 as Chevrolet's version of General Motors Corp.'s J cars, which included the Buick Skyhawk, Pontiac Sunbird and, at one point, the unbelievably silly

Complaints: Road noise	
Praise: An excellent commuter	
Head-turning Quotient: Zip, zip hooray!	
Ride, Acceleration, Handling: Decent	
Brakes: Standard anti-lock system	
Suggested Retail Price: $8,520	
Mileage: About 29 MPG	
U.S. Content: 90%	

Chevrolet Cavalier VL

Cadillac Cimarron (the best Chevrolet that Cadillac ever made).

The Cavalier and Sunbird survive in the J-car lineup, and will be on sale in the 1994-model year. Both cars are very decent, very reliable front-wheel-drive compacts capable of seating five people and carrying 13 cubic feet of cargo.

The Cavalier is sold as a coupe (two doors), sedan (four doors), wagon and convertible. Trim and performance packages include the base VL, upscale RS, and the top-of-the-line Z24, which is sold only as a coupe and convertible.

Complaints: No driver's air bag. Boo! Automatic safety belts — hate 'em!

Also, road noise is relatively high in the Cavalier VL, as it is in most economy subcompacts. The suspension is soft — but adequate. Just don't push the Cavalier VL the way you'd push a Pontiac Firebird or a Chevrolet Corvette. And, yeah, you've got to crank the windows up and down in this one.

Praise: The darned thing gets you where you're going in reasonable safety, particularly if you make sure that the manual lap-belts are latched in the "automatic" front seat-belt system. Practically all of the bugs have been worked out of the car, now going into its 12th year of production. The Cavalier VL does indeed represent good value for the money.

Head-turning quotient: Zip, zip, hooray!

Ride, acceleration, handling: Decent in all three categories. Brakes include power front discs and rear drums with a standard anti-lock braking system.

The test car was equipped with a standard 2.2-liter, four-cylinder, multi-port fuel injected engine rated 110 horsepower at 5,200 rpm. Maximum torque, twisting power, on that engine is 130 foot-pounds at 3,200 rpm.

An optional 3.1-liter V-6 engine, rated 140 horsepower at 4,200 rpm with max torque of 185 horsepower at 3,200 rpm, is available on Cavalier RS models. That engine is standard on the Cavalier Z24.

Mileage: About 29 to the gallon (15.2-gallon tank, estimated 431-mile range on usable volume of regular unleaded), running mostly highway and driver only with light cargo. Test car came with an optional, slightly whiny, three-speed automatic transmission. A more fuel-efficient five-speed manual is standard.

Sound system: Base four-speaker AM/FM stereo radio by GM/Delco. Great for listening to National Public Radio's "All things Considered" while cruising along Detroit's expressways.

Price note: The Cavalier VL's price is expected to hold steady at $8,520 in the 1994-model year, with the dealer's invoice sticking at $8,051. General Motors Corp. has pretty much paid for the tooling on these cars, which means that its making money on everyone it sells, which means that the company can afford to be a bit generous in using these models to build market share.

Coming changes: For 1994, the Chevrolet Cavalier gets a more gutsy 2.2-liter, in-line, four-cylinder engine. The new engine produces 120 horsepower at 5,200 rpm with a maximum torque of 130 foot-pounds at 4,000 rpm. Other changes include: redesigned rear brake drums; an improved wind-noise reduction package (a one-piece, window-to-door seal and an auxilliary seal in the door jamb); and standard power door locks and tinted glass on all Cavalier models.

Hometown: The Chevrolet Cavalier is assembled in Lordstown, Ohio.

CHEVROLET Corsica LT

Praise: A terrific value for the dollar

Head-turning Quotient: Nothing much

Ride, Acceleration, Handling: Decent

Brakes: Excellent

Suggested Retail Price: $11,400

Mileage: About 27 MPG

U.S. Content: 90%

The garage dudes shook their heads. They were disappointed. Over the years, I had entertained them weekly with one fancy car after another. Now, I was bringing them this — the Chevrolet Corsica LT sedan.

"Man, times must be rough," one of the garage attendants said, collecting the Corsica's keys.

"Oh, no!" said another attendant. "This can't be true. This ain't you. Where'd you get this jive car?"

I was caught off-guard. I'd grown fond of the Corsica LT during my week with the car. It was like a favorite sweater, not particularly attractive, but quite serviceable and comfortable. Also, considering its standard equipment and sticker price, it wouldn't be a bad deal for a money-pinched buyer.

I told the attendants this, and they gave me a hearing. But their faces said they weren't buying my line.

I picked up the car nine hours later. The brothers were still in a foul mood.

"Hey, man. Why are you getting on my case about this car?" I asked one of the attendants.

"Man, people like to dream," the attendant said. "You can't dream in no Corsica. That's a working man's car. Next time you bring a Chevrolet 'round here, you better bring a Corvette."

Background: The front-wheel-drive Corsica LT sedan, which has been around since the mid-1980s, was not made for fancy dreams. It was made for Middle America. It's a common-sense car, something to get you back and forth with maximum reliability and minimum hassle.

The car, which carries five people and 13.5 cubic feet of luggage, shows up everywhere — in shopping center parking lots and downtown garages, on Sunday streets outside of churches, in corporate automotive fleets and numerous working-class neighborhoods. Nowadays, with the U.S. economy still dragging tail, the Corsica is showing up in the parking lots of unemployment offices, too.

The Corsica LT sedan uses much of the same running gear found in the Cavalier. For 1994, it shares as standard equipment the Cavalier's 2.2-liter, four-cylinder, 120-horsepower engine. But the Corsica is a prettier shade of vanilla than its sibling; and it's 1.1-inches longer, nearly 2 inches wider, and almost 3 inches higher than the Cavalier.

The Corsica is sold as an LT sedan only. But, for 1994, it gets a new, optional 3.1-liter V-6 that sets it apart from the more workaday Cavalier. The new Corsica V-6 is rated 160-horsepower at 5,200 rpm with a maxi-

Chevrolet Corsica LT

mum torque of 185 foot-pounds at 4,000 rpm. The Corsica is mechanically identical to the Chevrolet Beretta, which is sold exclusively as a five-passenger coupe.

Complaint: On a tested 1992 Corsica LT, there was a distortion, a ripple-type thing in the lower-left side of the windshield. It was mildly bothersome. But the windshield of a rented 1993 Corsica LT was free of any distortion.

Praise: Driver's air bag is standard, as are anti-lock brakes. Overall, the Corsica LT represents terrific value for the dollar. Excellent fit and finish on the 1993 model.

Head-turning quotient: Turns nothing much. But it doesn't shock anyone with ugliness, either.

Ride, acceleration, handling: Very good ride. Good acceleration and decent handling. Again, this is a budget car that works fine when used within its limits. Braking setup also mirrors that of the Cavalier, power front discs/rear drums with anti-lock backup. Braking is excellent.

Please note that the tested 1992 and 1993 Corsica LT models were equipped with the then-standard, 2.2-liter, 110-horsepower, four-cylinder engine. Besides being a tad more powerful, the new 120-horsepower engine runs more quietly than its predecessor.

Sound system: Four-speaker AM/FM stereo radio and cassette by GM/Delco. Excellent economy boogie.

Overall, the Corsica LT represents terrific value for the dollar.

21

Mileage: As noted in the 1993 Corsica LT, about 27 miles per gallon (15.6 gallon tank, estimated 410-mile range on usable volume of regular unleaded), combined city-highway, running with one to four occupants and light cargo.

Both 1992 and 1993 Corsica LTs were equipped with standard five-speed manual transmissions.

Coming changes: Besides the improved four-cylinder engine and the new 3.1-liter V-6, the 1994 Corsica can also be equipped with GM's electronically controlled, four-speed automatic 4T60-E transmission, optional on V-6 models. Other changes include a redesigned front suspension and reworked rear brake drums, and standard air conditionining on all Corsica models.

Price note: The base price of the 1994 Corsica LT will hang at about $11,400, pretty close to its 1993 mark. Dealer's invoice will coast around $10,315.

Hometown: The Corsica LT is assembled in Wilmington, Del.

Complaints: Small seats; some engine lag

Praise: A spirited commuter

Head-turning Quotient: Wows the young'uns

Ride, Acceleration, Handling: Excellent

Suggested Retail Price: Nearly $12,000

Mileage: About 28 MPG

U.S. Content: 83%

FORD Escort GT

They stood there in blue-jeaned majesty, some wearing braces, others hiding pimpled faces, all certain of their intelligence, but none quite certain of what was before their eyes.

"This is an Escort?" one of the teenagers asked.

"Yes," I said.

"A Ford Escort?" he asked.

"Yes."

"But it's so, so..."

"Fresh," a girl said, finishing the boy's sentence.

That's "fresh" as in what "groovy" used to mean — hip, cool, acceptable in a vibrant sort of way. Neither word would have applied to an Escort in 1981, when the then-boxy, front-wheel-drive subcompact drove into the American market.

The first Escort was a best-seller, yeah. But it was a bestseller in the manner of laundry detergent and disposable kitchen towels. You didn't buy it because you loved it. You bought it because you needed it and, mostly, because it was all you could afford. And if you learned to love it, well, hey, even arranged marriages have their moments.

Ford Escort LX

Ford Motor Co. and its Japanese partner, Mazda Motor Corp., redesigned the Escort in 1991 and gave the car line, especially the tested Escort GT, something akin to libido.

Boxy lines were replaced with flippant curves. The cheap, make-do feel of the original Escort was upgraded with a quality touch. Young people, those consumer seedlings needed by companies to sustain future sales, looked at the car in 1991 and wanted it.

They're still looking at it with lust today.

Several trips to Virginia high schools in a teal-green 1993 Escort GT proved as much. Kids eyeballed the car. Others swarmed around it before morning classes. One student at Yorktown High School in Arlington, Va., paid it the highest compliment.

"Buy it for me, Dad," she said.

I told her, "No."

Background: The 1993 Escort GT and its sibling Escorts are hybrid cars that defy traditional notions of "American" automobiles. All Escorts are built on the subcompact Mazda Protege platform. Base and mid-line Escorts — including the LX hatchback, sedan and wagon — all share Ford's 1.9-liter, four-cylinder, fuel-injected engine, rated 88-horsepower at 4,400 rpm. Maximum torque is 108 foot-pounds at 3,800 rpm.

The Escort GT gets the Mazda-developed, 1.8-liter, four-cylinder, 16-valve job rated 127 horsepower at 6,500 rpm. The Mazda engine has a maximum torque of 114 foot-pounds at 4,500 rpm.

All Escorts are front-wheel-drive vehicles.

Complaints: The front and rear seats in the Escort GT are made for small, youthful behinds. Full-blown, adult derrieres just don't fit comfortably in this car. The five-speed manual in the tested 1993 Escort GT shifted smoothly enough; but there was still some engine lag, reminiscent of a discomfort in the 1991 model.

Praise: The Escort GT is a nicely styled, well-built, spirited subcompact — a nifty commuter that should please lots of owners. I loathe automatic seat belts. But they worked well in the 1993 Escort GT. Please use them in conjunction with the manual lap belts.

Head-turning quotient: Still wows the young'uns.

Ride, acceleration, handling: Excellent small-car ride. No brutal bumps and grinds. Great small-car handling. The Escort GT knows a curve when it sees one. Acceleration is good — could be better if the engine would match the transmission's rhythm.

Braking is good. The Escort GT is equipped with power four-wheel discs. No anti-lock brakes available at this writing.

Sound system: Four-speaker AM/FM stereo radio and cassette installed by Ford. Good boogie.

Mileage: About 28 to the gallon (11.9-gallon tank, estimated 323-mile range on usable volume of regular unleaded), mostly highway and driver only.

Price note: At nearly $12,000 with a dealer's invoice approaching $11,000, the Escort GT is a pricey econo-ride. That price gets higher with insurance, which carries a premium rating, largely because of the Escort GT's mostly youthful buyers, who don't rank well on the traffic-accident charts.

Coming changes: The 1994 Ford Escorts get a driver's air bag as standard equipment, something sorely needed by the little cars. Variable intermittent windhield wipers also come as standard equipment, along with a new air conditioner refrigerant, R134-A, that is supposed to do less harm to the earth's ozone layer. New 14-inch wheels and tires are standard on the 1994 Ford Escort wagon, and are optional on the three-door and four-door Escort LX models.

Hometown: The Escorts are made at Ford plants in Wayne, Mich. and Hermosillo, Mexico.

Honda Civic LX

HONDA Civic EX Sedan

It was another night of trying not to go crazy, which meant sitting around and talking about things we could not control: Crime. Drugs. Rising unemployment. Wars and rumors of holocaust. We talked a lot.

And when the talking was done, we left her apartment. It was a rhythmic departure marked by cadenced goodbyes and best wishes — and the sounds of cars starting in chilled midnight air.

I didn't crank the engine right away. I was driving the new Honda Civic EX, and there was something about the little car that prompted parked meditation. I liked its cabin — a tightly constructed, friendly place. I particularly like the car's instrument panel, with its big knobs and buttons, all well-placed and easy to use. The Civic EX sedan made sense — no small feat in a madcap world. And in making sense, the car provided hope.

Things done well lift the spirit. The Civic EX lifted mine. I cranked the engine and drove home.

Background: *Automobile Magazine*, the most literate of car-buff books, once called the Honda Civic "the world's best small car." I agreed with that 1992 assessment, and I continue to do so, with one caveat: The

Complaints: Poor sound system	
Praise: Everything	
Head-turning Quotient: Appealing	
Ride, Acceleration, Handling: All-around best	
Suggested Retail Price: About $15,500	
Mileage: About 33 MPG	
U.S Content: 60%	

front-wheel-drive Civic is the best small car as long as it's sold within bounds of the manufacturer's suggested retail price. The residual value of a Honda Civic — of any car, for that matter — drops in direct proportion to the amount of the dealer markup.

Think about it: Why should any used-car buyer pay you for your irrationality? If you dump an extra $2,000 on a dealer to get a car because that car is hot, that's your problem. Don't ask me to compensate you for your silliness three years down the road.

The Civic is hot, but it's not the only small car burning up the charts. There are legions of other high-quality, competitive small cars out there with value enhanced by sensible pricing.

There are seven Honda Civics in two basic groups: hatchback and sedan. The Civic sedans are built in the United States. Other Civic models are built in Canada and Japan.

All 1992 and 1993 Civics were equipped with driver-side air bags as standard equipment. *For 1994, all Civics get standard dual-front air bags. Also, anti-lock brakes will be available as standard equipment on many 1994 Civic models.* All of the new Civics have a bit more interior space than the pre-1992 cars. All are excellent subcompacts — within their suggested price range.

Complaints: Nothing that has anything to do with the quality, design, construction or presentation of the tested 1992 and 1993 Civic EX sedans.

Praise: Everything that relates to the quality, design, construction and presentation of the tested Civic EX sedans. It amazes me that Honda substantially has improved a car that already was darned good. Besides the driver-side air bag, other improvements include standard power four-wheel disc brakes with anti-lock backup; a quieter, smoother engine; a smoother, five-speed gearbox; an overall tighter body than pre-1992 models; a better suspension system.

Head-turning quotient: A front end that resembles every generic Japanese sedan, with hints of Mercedes-Benz 300 series styling in the rear. Honda blended the two styles into something that is distinctly, unequivocally Honda. Appealing.

Ride, acceleration, handling: All-around best in small-car category. The ride is excellent for four occupants. Credit the EX sedan's four-wheel-independent, double-wishbone suspension system. The car's bigger wheels — 14-inch diameter — also helped.

The EX sedan is equipped with a standard 1.6-liter, four-cylinder, 16-valve engine rated 125 horsepower at 6,600 rpm. Maximum torque is 105 foot-pounds at 5,200 rpm. The engine has variable-valve timing for optimum fuel efficiency.

Braking is excellent, especially on wet roads and in panic stops.

Sound system: Hmmmm. Did I say no complaints? Here's one. The

AM/FM stereo radio and cassette installed by Honda in both the 1992 and 1993 EX sedans were simply awful for listening to music. They were squawk boxes.

Mileage: In both the 1992 and 1993 sedans, mileage was about 33 miles per gallon (11.9-gallon tank, estimated 382-mile range on usable volume of regular unleaded). The test cars were equipped with standard, five-speed manual transmissions.

Coming changes: Besides standard dual-front air bags and a wider availability of anti-lock brakes, four engine choices are available for Honda Civics in 1994. The CX hatchback runs with a 1.5-liter, 70-horsepower, eight-valve, single overhead-cam four-cylinder engine. A 92-horsepower, 1.5-liter, 16-valve VTEC-E engine, also four-cylinder, goes into the VX hatchback. The DX hatchback and DX and LX sedans get a 102-horsepower version of the 1.5-liter VTEC. All Civic hot-runners — the Si and EX sedans, and the EX coupe — get the 125-horsepower, 1.6-liter, 16-valve VTEC.

Price note: Honda's prices have been moving, usually upward. Toward the end of the 1993-model year, the Civic EX sedan (with five-speed manual) carried a base price of $15,330 and a dealer's invoice of $13,031. The 1993 EX sedan with four-speed automatic transmission was priced at $16,080. Expect modest price increases in 1994.

Hometown: Civic EX sedans are assembled in East Liberty, Ohio.

MERCURY Topaz GS

With Notes on Ford Tempo

The Mercury Topaz is a chicken in every pot, guaranteed health care, a decent minimum wage. In short, it is motorized populism, one of the few new cars you can bring to a high-unemployment neighborhood without feeling guilty about having a job.

No one will think you're living the easy life in this one. How could they? Even in its Sunday clothes, such as the optional black luggage rack and seven-spoke aluminum wheels worn by the tested 1994 Topaz GS, the car has all of the elegance of a rolled brown bag.

That's not a slam. No way. Look at things in their context. Making it in the 1980s was symbolized by pinstripes and power meals. Making it today means eating at your desk.

Background: Time is running out for the Mercury Topaz and its like-

Complaints: Rough ride, velour interior

Praise: Inexpensive

Head-turning Quotient: Does not apply

Ride, Acceleration, Handling: Reasonable

Brakes: Decent

Suggested Retail Price: $10,900

Mileage: About 25 MPG

U.S. Content: 93%

Mercury Topaz GS

bodied cousin, the Ford Tempo. Those cars have been around since the fall of 1983. They will be replaced in the 1995-model year by versions of Ford Motor Co.'s "world car," the Mondeo, a front-wheel-drive sedan now on sale in Europe.

Ford has been showing off the Mondeo at car shows in the United States, whetting buyer appetites. At the same time, the company has been trimming offerings in its Topaz-Tempo line. For example, Topaz models no longer include the LS, LTS, and XR5 models. What remains are sedan and coupe versions of the Topaz GS.

That's not so bad. The Topaz GS is a decent commuter, one made more reliable than earlier Topaz models, thanks to the installation of a better fuel pump. (Fuel pumps in 1987-1989 Topaz-Tempo cars failed quite often.)

Also, the Topaz GS's suspension has been improved with reworked McPherson struts.

Complaints: Even with the suspension upgrade, the Topaz GS still sides rougher than many comparable compact cars. And, yechhh, that dorky velour interior! Take it away, please!

Praise: A decent, reasonably well-built car that could prove to be quite a bargain for someone in need of inexpensive wheels. A driver's air bag is optional on the Topaz GS.

Head-turning quotient: Does not apply.

Ride, acceleration, handling: Acceptable ride, decent acceleration, reasonably good handling. Look, this is a bread-and-butter car, nothing else. The standard engine in the tested 1994 Topaz GS is a 2.3-liter, inline four-cylinder job rated 96 horsepower at 4,200 rpm. Maximum torque is 126 foot-pounds at 2,600 rpm.

There is an optional 3-liter, V-6 engine rated 130 horsepower at 4,800 rpm with a maximum torque of 150 foot-pounds at 3,000 rpm.

Brakes include power front discs and rear drums — decent, reliable car stoppers. No anti-lock brakes were available at this writing.

Mileage: About 25 to the gallon (15.9-gallon tank, estimated 387-mile range on usable volume of regular unleaded). The test car was equipped with a three-speed automatic transmission.

Price note: Toward the end of the 1993-model year, the Topaz GS carried a base price of $10,900 and a dealer's invoice of $9,791. But dealers were discounting that price in 1993, and they're likely to continue discounting in 1994 to clear out any leftover Topaz-Tempo cars.

Coming changes: Fade to the left. Dim house lights. Close curtains. But first, add environmentally friendly refrigerant for 1994.

Hometown: The Topaz-Tempo cars are made in Kansas City, Mo.

MERCURY Tracer Wagon

They had gathered with hatches and tailgates open, waiting to accept the products of a Saturday's shopping at one of those ready-to-assemble furniture stores. There was a certain beauty to the scene — all of those trucks and station wagons neatly parked between diagonal lines. Only an occasional car broke the symmetry, but those of us with proper vehicles tried not to notice.

Propriety, in weekend visits to do-it-yourself emporiums, demands something like the Mercury Tracer station wagon. With its rear seats down, the little wagon becomes a mini-hog, consuming 66.9 cubic feet of cargo. The significance of such a bodacious performance can be measured only by the suffering of others, such as the couple — obviously newlyweds — trying to stuff several large boxes into the trunk of a Volkswagen Jetta passenger car.

Ah, smugness! It is knowing that you have the right set of wheels for

Complaints: Underpowered

Praise: Overall excellent quality

Ride, Acceleration, Handling: All very good, except for inadequate power under full load

Brakes: Decent

Suggested Retail Price: $10,982

Mileage: About 28 MPG

U.S. Content: 79%

Mercury Tracer Wagon

the right circumstance — a four-wheel-drive vehicle that gets you through the snow while others are slipping about, a super-duper sports car at a Southern California social event that does not involve guns or Molotov cocktails, and a neat little wagon for carrying bulky packages home from a furniture store. God, I love my job!

Background: The Tracer Wagon was remade in 1991 at the same time that Ford Motor Co. and Mazda Motor Corp got together to redo the practically identical Escort wagon and cars.

The Tracer remake included a bigger, peppier standard engine — an inline four-cylinder, 88-horsepower, 1.9-liter job (provided by Ford), compared with an 82-horsepower, 1.6-liter version in the pre-1991 Tracers.

Like the redone Escorts, the Tracers are base on the Mazda Protege platform.

Complaints: With its air conditioner going and its cargo bay loaded to the max, the Tracer wagon's engine became a wheezy thing, a machine flirting with an asthma attack. Cutting off the air conditioner improved engine breathing and performance.

Praise: Overall excellent small-car quality. Some economy cars feel cheap. The Tracer wagon feels rich without the wannabe paste-ons — the gewgaws, automatic this and that, and fancy wheels — that some manufacturers routinely add to economy cars to make them feel and sell "upscale."

Head-turning quotient: Everybody mistook the Tracer wagon for the bigger, pricier Mercury Sable wagon. Some Ford marketing people were pleased by that public reaction.

"That's what we wanted," one company official said. Uhmm-hmm. I wonder what the Sable buyers think about that.

Ride, acceleration, handling: Very good on all fronts, with the notable exception of the 1.9-liter, four-cylinder engine's less-than-stellar performance under full load.

Braking, a matter of power front discs and rear drums, was decent. Panic breaking was better with the cargo bay loaded. In lightly loaded condition, panic braking in the Tracer wagon was noticeably more skittish.

Mileage: About 28 to the gallon (11.9-gallon tank, estimated 323-mile range on usable volume of regular unleaded), combined city-highway, running with one to two occupants and an occasional use of air conditioner, including several trips carrying cargo in excess of 400 pounds.

The test wagon was equipped with an optional four-speed automatic transmission. A five-speed manual is standard.

Sound system: Four-speaker AM/FM stereo radio and cassette, installed by Ford. Very decent.

Price note: Base price on the Tracer Wagon toward the end of the 1993-model year was $10,982 with a dealer invoice of $9,863. Prices will hang around this mark for 1994. Many dealers selling Tracers and Escorts have been participating in a hassle-saving, cost-saving (assuming that time is money), single-price or "best buy" program. Check with your local dealer.

Coming changes: The 1994 Mercury Tracer Wagon gets a standard driver's air bag, 120-mph speedometer, new seat fabrics, upgraded door trim panels, and a new AM/FM radio. The wagon can be equipped with an optional 1.8-liter, double-overhead cam, inline four-cylinder engine rated 127 horsepower at 6,500 rpm with a maximum torque of 114 foot-pounds at 4,500 rpm.

Hometown: The Mercury Tracer is assembled in Hermosillo, Mexico.

Overall excellent small-car quality.

NISSAN Sentra SE-R

The Nissan Sentra proves that mediocrity can rise above itself. In many ways, it is an excellent subcompact, far superior to its original incarnation

Nissan Sentra SE-R

Complaints: Road noise	
Praise: A delight. Ample space for adults, even in the rear seats	
Head-turning Quotient: Ho, hum	
Ride, Acceleration, Handling: Very good	
Brakes: Excellent	
Suggested Retail Price: $13,470	
Mileage: About 28 MPG	
U.S. Content: 60%	

in 1982, which was a tinny, unsubstantial thing.

Indeed, the first Sentra was insulting in its banality. The new Sentra, particularly the SE-R version, has a different attitude. It has a sense of pride, a dignity of purpose — which is to provide as much fun, quality and practicality as possible in an affordable, attractive family car.

Nissan's designers obviously cared about what they were doing with the two-door, front-wheel-drive Sentra SE-R. Its body is rounded and friendly. The interior is simple and well-designed. Overall, there is a richness about the passenger cabin that belies the Sentra's roots as an econobox.

Background: The Sentra car line was substantially reworked in 1991, resulting in the models currently on sale in America. More upgrades were done in 1993 — new taillamps and rear fascia, new headlamps and grille.

The first Sentra cars were built in Japan. The new models are made in the United States. Sentras are available as two-door coupes in E (base), XE, SE, and SE-R trim. Sedans come in E, XE, and GXE trim.

People looking for true family cars should shop one of the four-door models. Young couples and singles, short on cash but long on desire for a quality car with personality, should check out one of the Sentra coupes.

All Sentras are front-wheel-drive.

Complaints: Road noise, common to most subcompact and compact cars. Peripheral vision somewhat impeded by design of A-pillars — the pillars that form the vertical frame for the windshield.

Praise: It's nice to climb into an economy car that delights instead of depresses. The doors of the tested SE-R close with a "thunk." The two front seats are very comfortable, even for middle-aged butts and backs. In the rear, there is ample space for two adults.

A driver air bag is standard on the Sentra GXE, but optional on other models. Anti-lock brakes are available for the SE-R and GXE.

Head-turning quotient: The Sentra SE-R scored high on the wow-factor chart when it was introduced in 1991. But now, caught in a tidal wave of highly attractive, competitive models, the SE-R gets about as much notice as driftwood.

Ride, acceleration and handling: Excellent — but no longer distinctively good. The competition thing, again. The ride is smooth, thanks to the four-wheel-independent suspension system. The SE-R's brakes, standard four-wheel discs, are excellent. The tested 1993 SE-R was equipped with optional anti-lock brakes.

Acceleration is whammo! The SE-R comes with a standard 2-liter, inline four-cylinder, 16-valve engine rated 140 horsepower at 6,400 rpm, with a maximum torque of 132 foot-pounds at 4,800 rpm.

The standard engine in the other Sentras is a 1.6-liter, inline four rated 110 horsepower at 6,000 rpm, with a maximum torque of 108 foot-pounds at 4,000 rpm.

Mileage: About 28 to the gallon (13.2-gallon tank, estimated 360-mile range on usable volume of regular unleaded), city-highway, carrying one to four occupants and light cargo. The test car had a five-speed manual transmission.

Price note: The Sentra SE-R ended the 1993 model year with a base price of $13,470 and a dealer's invoice of $11,885. Again, prices on Japanese name-plate cars have been rising, regardless of place of manufacture. But buyers can expect price moderation on the Sentra, inasmuch as Nissan is trying to give the car a fighting chance of making a go of it in an extremely crowded U.S. small-car market.

Hometown: The Nissan Sentra cars are made in Smyrna, Tenn.

Plymouth Sundance Duster

PLYMOUTH Sundance Duster

With Notes on the Dodge Shadow and Chrysler Neon

Sometimes, nostalgia is best left in a closet, or packed away in a box in the corner of an attic, or buried in files. Such interments give dignity to memories by covering them with myths.

But we are, many of us, so desperate to grab ahold of dreams of better times, we're forever digging into our past and pulling out symbols of perfection. It's the "Brady Bunch" syndrome.

Problem is, nothing was ever that good — not TV's 1970s "Brady Bunch" as the epitome of American family life, nor the 1970s Plymouth Duster as a sterling example of U.S. automotive prowess.

The "Brady Bunch" was a fake. The 1970s Duster, particularly Duster 340, was just another American road hog outfitted with a big ol' V-8 engine.

Still, both the TV show and the car had a certain charm, a kind of happy funk that became funkier with age and distance. But the nostalgia merchants couldn't leave well enough alone. They destroyed the halo of the "Brady Bunch" by giving us remakes and updates featuring the show's once youthful stars in various stages of middle-aged distress. Now, they've gone and tarnished the gilded memories of the Duster by giving us the dramatically underwhelming and somewhat cheap Plymouth Sundance Duster, introduced in 1992.

Background: First, let's say this: As economy cars, the front-wheel-drive Plymouth Sundance and its identical twin, the Dodge Shadow, are among the best and most reasonably priced available. Even with their base, 93-horsepower, 2.2-liter, inline four-cylinder engines, they come well-equipped. Throw in the optional single-overhead cam, 100-horsepower, 2.5-liter in-line four, mix it with the standard five-speed manual transmission, and you've really got a super econocar deal. Hey, those cars come with a standard driver's air-bag, too.

But the Duster version of the Sundance, with its three-liter 141-horsepower V-6, is a motorized malaprop — an econocar with muscle-car pretensions meant to appeal to teenagers in tight jeans living on tight budgets.

As such, the Duster flirts with marketing cynicism, the belief that young folks will fall for anything if it's flashy and hyped enough. Sadly, it appears that Plymouth's marketers are right. Since the introduction of the "new" Duster in 1992, Sundance sales have risen dramatically.

Complaints: The Sundance Duster feels made-up, fake. It's a feeling heightened by the practically useless "air spoiler" atop the trunk lid and the amusement-park-like "Duster" logos painted on the car's exterior.

Add to that the undamped noise of the V-6 (141-horsepower at 5,000 rpm/171 foot-pounds torque at 2,400 rpm) coming through the Duster's petite little body, and you've got a case of roaring status discrepancy.

Praise: The Plymouth Sundance is far, far better as an economy car than it is as a wannabe hot-rod. Driver's air bag is standard in the Duster. Anti-lock brakes are optional. Get them.

Head-turning quotient: In the words of one of my parking attendants: "This 'Duster' ain't nothin' but a Sundance with a bump on the hood. Totally jive!"

Ride, acceleration, handling: Average ride. Excellent acceleration. Squirmy handling — the front end felt out of control (characteristic of both the 1992 and 1993 Dusters I drove). Braking is good. The tested Sundance Dusters were equipped with standard power front discs and rear drums. The 1992 model came without anti-lock backup. An optional anti-lock system was installed in the 1993 test car.

Mileage: As noted in the 1993 model, equipped with a standard five-speed manual transmission, about 24 miles to the gallon (14-gallon tank, estimated 326-mile range on usable volume of regular unleaded), combined city-highway, driver only.

Price note: Toward the end of the 1993-model year, the two-door Duster had a base price of $10,498, with a dealer's invoice of $9,478. Four-door models were about $400 higher on the sticker and the dealer's

Complaints: Underwhelming

Praise: Far better as an economy car than as a wannabe hot-rod

Head-turning Quotient: Totally jive!

Ride, Acceleration, Handling: Fair to middlin'

Brakes: Get the optional anti-lock system

Suggested Retail Price: $10,498

Mileage: About 24 MPG

U.S. Content: 90%

invoice. Regular Plymouth Sundance cars were selling under $9,000. I expect these prices to hold in the 1994-model year.

Coming changes: Chrysler Corp. is about to revamp most of its small-car line with the introduction of its PL cars, led by the Chrysler Neon, in January 1994. The Neon, which will be the first subcompact car featuring dual front air bags, will go on sale as a 1995 model at a base price of $8,600. The front-wheel-drive car will be powered by a 2-liter, 16-valve, four-cylinder engine.

Assuming that Chrysler does as good a job with its small PL cars as it did with the splendid, mid-size LH models introduced in 1993, the likelihood is that the Sundance soon will dance into the sunset; the Dodge Shadow will move permanently into the shadows; and the Duster will take a well-deserved trip to the dustbin. But, before the Sundance / Shadow / Duster do their collective fade, they will get a few fixes for 1994. Those include an improved four-speed automatic transmission, non-chloroflourocarbon (CFC) R-134A air conditioner refrigerant, improved seat-belt buckles and a knee bolster for the right-front passenger.

Hometowns: The Sundance/Shadow cars are made at Chrysler assembly plants in Sterling Heights, Mich., and Toluca, Mexico.

Complaints: Road noise
Praise: An excellent commuter
Head-turning Quotient: Cute. No rush
Ride, Acceleration, Handling: Decent
Brakes: Excellent
Suggested Retail Price: $11,4195
Mileage: About 32 MPG
U.S. Content: 98%

SATURN SC1 Coupe

It was a ceremony of motorized incompetence, a feast of error, a rolling carnival of selfishness. It's a wonder no one was killed.

The occasion was a regular commute, a five-hour drive from New York to Washington, conducted along the New Jersey Turnpike and Interstate-95. The day was rain soaked. The traffic was hell. I was driving the 1993 Saturn SC1 coupe, which was the only decent thing about the trip.

"Decent" needs emphasis. The word here means acceptable, good, meeting an honorable standard, meeting expectations. It does not mean exceptional. But "decent" was okay on this day when seemingly everyone on the road, myself included, had fallen into a decidedly indecent mood.

I first noticed something amiss when a dingy, red Nissan Sentra skittered across the turnpike into the left lane, where the Nissan's driver proceeded to tailgate a white Ford Taurus, whose operator apparently had taken up residence in that section of the highway. This dance of intimida-

Saturn SC1 Coupe

tion continued until it became a threesome, foursome and more — with vehicle after vehicle stacking up behind the Taurus, whose driver refused to relinquish the passing lane.

Naturally, there was a reaction to all of this. Impatient drivers swung from behind the Taurus, often without signaling, and then zipped into the middle lane, then zoomed into the right lane, and then raced back across the rain-slicked pavement to the left lane from whence they came. All of that frenetic movement got the impatient ones three or four car lengths ahead of the Taurus.

Heavy trucks joined the party near the southbound end of the New Jersey Turnpike and stayed for much of the journey along I-95 South. The little Saturn SC1 was holding up pretty good, but I wasn't. I lost it, and did a stupid thing.

A big hugga-mugga of a truck swooped down on me in the middle lane. So, I moved to the right. The truck moved to the right lane right behind me. I got mad and dropped my speed from the mid-60s to 55 miles per hour. The middle lane was blocked with traffic. The truck had nowhere to go. In retrospect, I'm glad that big truck had good brakes.

Background: Saturn Corp. is entering its fourth year of production and, by most accounts, is doing reasonably well. The General Motors Corp. small-car subsidiary continues to post strong sales, which should help it come close to breaking even at the end of calendar-year 1993. If strong

A nicely done,

sporty, front-

wheel-drive

economy coupe.

sales and cost-cutting continue, Saturn is a sure bet to break-even and, perhaps, become profitable in 1994.

Saturn will need those profits.

To help keep costs down, and keep money in the bank, the company has been forced to delay redesign of its sedans and wagons until the 1996-model year. It has also pushed back a restyling of its coupe until model-year 1997. Originally, Saturn officials had planned to do a 1995-model-year facelift on its sedans and wagons, and a 1996 update of its coupe.

However, Saturn is on track for a 1995 interior remake of its coupe, sedans, and wagons. That inside job will bring about a new dashboard with dual front air bags, new seat belts, and improved dials and controls.

But, for the moment, what Saturn has is all right.

The SC1 coupe, introduced in 1993, is a nicely done, sporty, front-wheel-drive economy coupe. The test model came with a standard five-speed manual transmission; a 1.9-liter, inline four-cylinder engine rated 85 horsepower at 5,000 rpm, with a maximum torque of 107 foot-pounds at 2,400 rpm; and enough space for four "normal-size" adults and 11.3 cubic feet of cargo.

A more spiffy, zippy Saturn coupe — the SC2 with a 124-horsepower inline four — is available.

Complaints: Road noise is a problem in the SC1 But you can live with it, especially on smooth roads where the noise level declines. Also, the plastic-bodied Saturn can be bullied by cross-winds on interstates.

Praise: The SC1 is an excellent commuter, particularly if the commutes are 50 miles or less. It is a well-made, competent little car that also does well in the snow. A driver's air bag is standard.

Head-turning quotient: Cute. No rush. No flush. Just cute.

Ride, acceleration, handling: Decent marks in all categories, a car that gives the reasonable performance it is designed to give. Brakes on the test model were optional power four-wheel discs with anti-lock backup. Braking was excellent.

Standard brakes are power front discs/rear drums. Traction control, designed to prevent wheel slippage when starting from stop on slippery surfaces, is available in Saturn cars (except the SL sedan) equipped with optional four-speed automatic transmissions.

Mileage: Very good, about 32 to the gallon (12.8-gallon tank, estimated 400-mile range on usable volume of regular unleaded), running mostly highway with one to two occupants.

Sound system: Four-speaker, AM/FM stereo radio and cassette by GM/Delco — excellent during low-speed drives; but it becomes a voice whining in the distance in heavy, high-speed traffic.

Price note: Toward the end of the 1993-model year, the tested SC1 coupe had a suggested retail price of $11,195 with a dealer's invoice of

$9,852. Saturn cars received modest price boosts in 1993, and probably will receive a few more in 1994. No-haggle Saturn selling, appreciated by many car shoppers, is expected to remain in place.

Ah, yes: Check with your insurer on the SC1 coupe. In fact, check with your insurer before buying ANY sports coupe, especially if you are single, male, and under 25 years old. Folks in that category tend to be involved in more than their fair share of injurious and fatal crashes. Folks in that demographic range who drive sports coupes tend to have even worse records. Insurance companies set their rates accordingly. Thus, fair or not, the Saturn coupe carries a premium rate.

Late flash! **Warning:** If your Saturn car or wagon was built before April 15, 1993, it is subject to an important voluntary recall. A portion of the generator wiring harness in those models can overheat and lead to underhood fires. No deaths or injuries have been reported as a result of this defect; and Saturn, much to its credit, has mounted an aggressive recall campaign to help ensure that none of its customers gets hurt. Under rare circumstances, some affected Saturn customers are eligible for new cars or wagons. Check with your dealer for details.

Hometown: Saturn cars are made in Spring Hill, Tenn.

SATURN SW2 Wagon

Complaints: Road noise, automatic seat belts
Praise: Good quality at a reasonable price
Head-turning Quotient: A heartthrob
Ride, Acceleration, Handling: Generally excellent
Suggested Retail Price: $13,070
Mileage: About 31 MPG
U.S. Content: 98%

It was a little wagon. So, when I saw the kid's pile of stuff, I shouted: "No way!" But she insisted, and loaded the thing with two duffel bags of fresh laundry, a floor lamp, computer, printer, victuals, pots and pans, books, tapes, compact discs, blankets and God knows what else. Surprisingly, there was enough room left in the Saturn wagon for three bodies. We departed our Virginia homestead and headed north toward New York.

More surprises came en route. For example, even stacked and packed, the 1993 Saturn SW2 wagon was comfortable. Before reaching Delaware, both the kid and my helpmate had fallen asleep — one snoozing in what space remained on a rear seat, and the other doing the zzzz-thing in the front passenger's seat.

Another stunner was the wagon's performance. The little thing could run. It survived the brutalities of turnpikes and expressways by scooting out of danger whenever necessary. It stopped smartly in panic situations, and moved around New York City's myriad potholes with admirable dex-

Saturn SW2 Wagon

terity.

We finally made it to the kid's dormitory on the West Side of New York. "Wow," she said, waking as we pulled up to her dorm door. "We're here, already?"

Background: Say what you will about former General Motors Corp. Chairman Roger B. Smith. Beat him up for not moving fast enough to cut GM's costs, or for moving too slowly, in many instances, to meet rapidly changing consumer demands. But give him credit for bringing Saturn Corp. into play.

Now entering its fourth year, Saturn continues to set standards for customer treatment and small-car quality. It's become America's preeminent no-hassle car company — no hassle on the showroom floor, no hassle in the repair shop and, mostly, no hassle on the road. The upshot is that Saturn has been pulling in tens of thousands of customers, 50 percent of whom have said in surveys that they would've bought a Japanese-nameplate car (one made by a Japanese company, but not necessarily an import) had Saturn not existed.

That's pretty good testimony considering that the competition in question includes the likes of the Honda Civic, Subaru Impreza, Toyota Corolla/Prizm, and Mazda Protege/Escort/Tracer.

The magic here is common sense: offer people a decent, likable car at a reasonable price. Treat them with respect. Promptly take care of their legitimate gripes. They will buy.

Like Saturn's sedans and coupes, the wagons are front-wheel-drive, plastic-bodied vehicles capable of carrying four people. They are the high-quality economy cars that many people thought America could not build. Ol' Roger, for all of his faults, believed Americans could compete in that category. He was right.

Complaints: Road noise, which haunts most small cars and wagons. Also, all Saturn vehicles come with standard driver's air bags. I just wish they came with standard, manual lap and shoulder harnesses to complement the bag. Instead, Saturn has chosen to go with those irritating "automatic" front seat belts — the kind that slide along the interior roof perimeter whenever you open or close the front doors, the kind that always seem to catch you by the neck or slap you in the face. Hate 'em!

Praise: Good quality, decent styling, good engineering at a reasonable price. The Saturn SW2 wagon is not a gee-whiz mobile. It's not supposed to be. It's solid family transportation, only slightly larger in overall dimensions than Saturn sedans.

The Ford Escort and Toyota Corolla wagons have more cargo space than the Saturn wagon's allotted 28.8 cubic feet with the rear seats up and 56.3 cubic feet with rear seats down. But what's there in the Saturn is quite sufficient for most family runs.

Head-turning quotient: Heartthrob among current Saturn owners and many prospective buyers of small wagons.

Ride, acceleration and handling: Generally excellent marks all around.

Handling demerit: With its cargo area empty, the Saturn wagon gets blown about the highway in high winds. You can still control the wagon okay, but you have to concentrate.

Acceleration is good. The SW2 wagon comes with a standard 1.9-liter, 16-valve, double-overhead cam, fuel-injected, inline four-cylinder engine rated 124 horsepower at 5,600 rpm, with a maximum torque of 122 foot-pounds at 2,800 rpm. The Saturn SW1 wagon comes with a single-overhead cam, 85-horsepower version of that engine.

The tested SW2 was equipped with Saturn's optional braking system — power four-wheel discs with anti-lock backup. Standard brakes include power front discs/rear drums.

The test model also had the optional traction-control system.

Mileage: About 31 to the gallon (12.8-gallon tank, estimated 390-mile range on usable volume of regular unleaded gasoline), mostly highway, running with three occupants and about 350 pounds of cargo.

Sound system: Four-speaker AM/FM stereo radio and cassette with optional compact disc player, by GM/Delco. Okay boogie.

Price note: Toward the end of the 1993 model year, the SW2 wagon with automatic transmission had a base suggested retail price of $13,070 and a dealer's invoice of $11,371. Saturn prices have been edging up, and probably will continue to creep upward in 1994.

Coming changes: Not much for 1994. Some key interior changes, including dual front air bags, are planned for 1995.

Late flash! **Warning:** As indicated in the Saturn SC1 Coupe review, all Saturn cars and wagons built before April 15, 1993, are subject to an important voluntary recall. A defect in the generator wiring harness can cause underhood fires in those models. No deaths or injuries related to the defect have been reported at this writing. Please check with your Saturn dealer for details.

Hometown: Saturn wagons are assembled in Spring Hill, Tenn.

Complaints: Manual mirrors
Praise: Zippy — and quiet too
Head-turning Quotient: Pleasantly boring
Ride, Acceleration, Handling: Decent
Brakes: Excellent
Suggested Retail Price: $12,978
Mileage: About 30 MPG
U.S. Content: 60%

TOYOTA Corolla DX Wagon

The talk was about Bill Clinton, and whether he would do something to encourage people to buy the kind of vehicle that was bringing us home from New York. It was a rolling forum, held in a 1993 Toyota Corolla DX wagon, loaded with three college students and their undone laundry.

Consensus gave thumbs up to the compact wagon, which was surprisingly comfortable and quiet. But Clinton got a round of raspberries from the traveling scholars, who couldn't understand how the President expects to save gas by selling it below world-market prices.

"Doesn't make sense," said Arden, a Columbia senior majoring in economics. "He wants people to use less gasoline, but he doesn't want a gas tax. Why would people use less of what they can get cheap?"

Binta, the musician-turned-aspirant lawyer, had another question: "Would people buy fuel-efficient vehicles if they had to pay more for gas?"

Empirical observation at turnpike gas pumps offered an answer: Maybe. Price-sensitive buyers, many of them home-bound students, seemed content to run the road in small vehicles such as the Corolla DX wagon. Also, the small-car drivers seemed less inclined to say, "Fill 'er up!"

But there were far more gas hogs than fuel-sippers at the pumps. There were big sport-utility vehicles and vans, plenty of mid-size and full-size sedans, and a good sampling of thirsty sports cars, many of which were sucking up premium unleaded at less than $1.50 a gallon.

Tony, one of the few college dudes I know who actually wants to be a

Toyota Corolla DX Wagon

teacher, thought there was a lesson in what we saw at the service stations.

"People want things that are good for the environment as long as someone else pays to get them," he said, which made me laugh. I was thinking about the dirty laundry we were hauling home from New York.

Background: Toyota's Corollas are no longer subcompact vehicles. Both the Corolla car and wagon have grown to compact models, providing more space for passengers and cargo. Still, these front-wheel-drive machines remain economy vehicles, though a buyer's yen for options can push them into the pricey range.

The Corolla wagon is sold only in DX trim (a step above Standard). It is equipped with a 1.8-liter, inline four-cylinder, 16-valve engine rated 115 horsepower at 5,600 rpm, with a maximum torque of 115 foot-pounds at 2,800 rpm.

Complaints: Manually operated sideview mirrors on the tested DX wagon. I hate 'em. They're a pain to adjust.

Praise: I expected the wagon — because it is a wagon — to be a lot less fun to drive than the Corolla sedan. I was wrong. Even loaded with people and cargo, the five-passenger DX wagon zipped along turnpikes and moved through traffic with admirable rhythm. And the thing was reasonably quiet. Flush body edges and exterior moldings, tighter-fitting doors and the use of foam rubber in the DX wagon's body cavities helped to keep noise under control.

Really impressive handling, especially under load.

For 1994, dual-front air bags are standard on all Corolla models. In addition, the wagons come with very decent cargo space — 31.4 cubic feet with the rear seats up, and nearly double that with the rear seats down.

Head-turning quotient: Pleasantly boring.

Ride, acceleration, handling: Overall excellence. Really impressive handling, especially under load. Credit the wagon's four-wheel-independent suspension system, outfitted with McPherson struts and stabilizer bars front and rear.

Braking is excellent. Brakes include ventilate front discs and rear drum with optional anti-lock backup.

Mileage: About 30 to the gallon (13.2-gallon tank, estimated 384-mile range on usable volume of regular unleaded), mostly highway, running with four occupants and about 400 pounds of cargo. The test DX wagon was equipped with an optional four-speed automatic transmission.

Sound system: Four-speaker AM/FM stereo radio and cassette with optional compact disc, installed by Toyota. Excellent.

Price note: Toward the end of the 1993-model year, the base price on the Corolla DX wagon was $12,978, with a dealer's invoice of $11,160. Again, prices on Japanese-nameplate cars have been rising. Expect modest increases on Corolla DX wagons in 1994.

Coming changes: Besides dual-front air bags, the 1994 Corolla Wagon gets the environmentally friendly R-134A air conditioner refrigerant and improved safety belts to simplify the installation of child-safety seats.

Hometowns: Toyota Corolla models are assembled in Fremont, Calif. by New United Motor Manufacturing, Inc., a joint venture operated by Toyota Motor Corp. and General Motors Corp. Corolla models also are assembled in Cambridge, Ontario, by Toyota Motor Manufacturing Canada Inc.

TOYOTA Corolla LE Sedan

With a Discussion of the Practically Identical Geo Prizm

Paul had one, and I think his was yellow. It was a Toyota Corolla sedan, I remember that much. Paul, a buddy of mine from life on another newspaper, always bragged about his Corolla. To hear him tell it, the little car could climb mountains and ford streams and still run for two weeks on the same tank of gas. The more abuse the car took, the more my friend boasted.

But when Paul became richer than his newspaper salary, he ditched

Toyota Corolla LE Sedan

his Corolla. Then, again, maybe he ditched it when the first kid came. Nahh, come to think of it, maybe his first wife took the car after Paul ditched her. What can I say? The memory gets fogged.

Bottom line is that the Corolla sedan would've lasted forever, or so it seemed, had circumstances in Paul's life not changed. It was a relatively simple compact car, rear-wheel-drive in those days, built to run long and cheaply. That's why so many Corollas, more than three million in all, have been sold in this country since their introduction in 1968. More than 80 percent of those Corollas are still on the road, according to Toyota Motor Corp.

Which brings me back to Paul: Last time I saw him, he was a high-flying public relations dude for somebody's Wall Street company. He looked prosperous, way too prosperous for the likes of a Corolla, which is too bad. A new line of Corollas went on sale in 1993; and will remain in the market, with some minor changes, in 1994.

The new Corollas are bigger, better, and safer than their predecessors. I've spent lots of time in these cars, especially the top-line Corolla LE sedan. I think that the old Paul would've liked it.

Then again, with the last few years being the unkindest of times on Wall Street, where so many people aren't doing as well as once before, the new Paul might like it, too.

Background: Toyota changed its Corolla cars to front-wheel-drive in

Complaints: Misleading advertising

Praise: A good, solid economy car

Head-turning Quotient: Another work of pleasant boredom

Ride, Acceleration, Handling: Very good in all three categories

Brakes: Excellent

Suggested Retail Price: $15,218

Mileage: About 30 MPG

U.S. Content: 60%

1984. That was a big gamble with cars that had done so well as rear-wheel-drive models. But the front-wheel-drive Corollas were a hit. Still, last year, Toyota rolled the dice again.

The company changed the cramped, subcompact Corolla into a more accommodating compact car. That means four normal adults can sit in the new car without going through the sardine routine. It also means they have more space for luggage and other cargo.

Other 1993 improvements to the Corolla included front seats mounted on the center tunnel and side rail, thus giving rear-seat passengers more foot room; adjustable seat-belt anchors; standard driver's air bag; and a more extensive use of galvanized steel.

In addition to the tested LE, the new Corollas include the Standard sedan and the better-appointed DX sedan and, of course, the Corolla DX wagon.

Complaints: Nothing to do with the quality of the product. But I am ticked off with a lot of misleading Toyota dealer advertising surrounding the Corolla — advertising that proclaims loudly and wrongly that there is a substantial difference between the Corolla and the Geo Prizm sold by Toyota's American partner, General Motors Corp.

For the record: There is no substantial difference between the Corolla and the Prizm. Here's why:

• Both cars are made in the same California plant by the same manufacturer, New United Motor Manufacturing Inc., a joint-venture company operated by Toyota and GM.

• Both cars are based on the same platform, with minor alterations in sheet metal and interior appointments.

• Both cars share much of the same running gear — standard 1.6-liter, 16-valve, inline four-cylinder engines rated 105-horsepower at 5,800 rpm, with a maximum torque of 100 foot-pounds at 4,800 rpm in the base models. Both come with standard five-speed manual transmissions in the base models.

• Most certainly, both are subject to the same rigid quality-assurance standards at the NUMMI plant.

The differences between the Corolla and Prizm, such as they exist, are these:

• The Corolla is available as a wagon. (GM is overloaded with wagons, and *does not need* the Corolla wagon in its lineup.)

• On its DX sedan and wagon, Toyota offers as standard equipment a 1.8-liter, 16-valve, inline four-cylinder engine rated 115 horsepower at 5,600 rpm, with a maximum torque of 115 foot-pounds at 2,800 rpm. That engine is optional on the Geo Prizm.

• Because of erroneous buyer perceptions, chiefly that "Japanese" cars are inherently superior to "American" automobiles, buyers generally pay

The Corolla has always been a good, solid economy car. The new Corolla/Prizm is even better.

less on the front end to get into the Geo Prizm, but get more on the back side when they sell or trade in their Corolla (the idea here being that the Corolla somehow, magically, does a better job of retaining its value). But those perceptions are likely to change as more consumers become aware of the growing interrelationships between Japanese and American auto makers, and the parity in quality between American and foreign automobiles.

Praise: The Corolla has always been a good, solid economy car. The new Corolla/Prizm is even better.

Head-turning quotient: The Corolla was never pretty. The new Corolla isn't pretty, either. Stylistically, it's another work of pleasant boredom.

Ride, acceleration, handling: Very good in all three categories. The tested Corolla LE sedan comes with the 1.8-liter, inline four-cylinder engine as standard equipment.

Brakes in the tested Corolla LE include ventilated front discs and rear drums with an optional anti-lock backup. Braking is excellent.

Mileage: About 30 to the gallon (13.2-gallon tank, estimated 390-mile range on usable volume of regular unleaded), combined city-highway, running with one to four occupants and light cargo.

The Corolla LE comes with a standard, four-speed automatic transmission. That transmission is optional on the Prizm. A three-speed automatic, to go along with the 1.6-liter engine, is available for both the Corolla and the Prizm.

Sound system: Four-speaker AM/FM stereo radio and cassette with compact disc, electronically controlled, installed by Toyota. Excellent.

Coming changes: For 1994, both Corolla and Prizm models get dual-front air bags, ozone-friendly R-134A air conditioner refrigerant, improved seat belts for better child-safety seat installation, and some new exterior paint jobs.

Price note: Toward the end of the 1993-model year, the Corolla LE sedan had a base price of $15,218, with a dealer's invoice of $13,042. The comparable Geo Prizm LSi sedan had a base price of $10,745 and a dealer's invoice of $9,907. Keep in mind that the Corolla LE comes with the larger 1.8-liter engine and the four-speed automatic transmission, and a few other goodies, as standard equipment. But even when those items are added as optional equipment to the GM Prizm LSi version, buyers still tend to come out ahead with the Prizm.

Again, note that prices on Japanese-nameplate cars have been rising, regardless of place of manufacture. That's partly because Japanese auto makers have been trying to retain profitability in an era of unfavorable foreign-exchange rates affecting the Japanese yen. Best advice: Shop around on this one — making sure that you compare the features and prices of the Corolla and Prizm, both of which are super high-quality compact cars.

Hometown: The Corolla and Prizm sedans are made by New United Motor Manufacturing Inc., a Toyota-GM joint-venture company in Fremont, Calif.

2

When Ozzie Met Harriet

BUICK Regal Gran Sport

With Notes on Chevrolet Lumina, Pontiac Grand Prix,
Oldsmobile Cutlass Supreme

It's 5 a.m. in a chain-hotel room, one of those cookie-cutter cubicles in which predictability has been raised to the status of virtue. I detest the place, but I'm seduced by its brazen consistency, which is more than I can say for the Buick Regal Gran Sport sedan I left at home. What a maddeningly disconsonant machine!

The car has the body of a two-door sports coupe; it would look better as such. But two more doors have been added to make it more attractive to families. The result is something that has the aesthetic appeal of a double-bed hotel room in which two cots have been added to accommodate extra guests.

For 1993, the Regal Gran Sport's body has been touched up — new grille and headlamps, new taillamps and bumpers — to give it the illusion of modern design. But that illusion is betrayed by the dated reality of the car's interior, which can best be described as eclectic dysfunction. The instrument panel, for example, is a recessed ribbon of tiny analog gauges, all improperly placed — a condition manifested by a speedometer tucked far away to the left.

Complaints: Eclectic dysfunctional interior

Praise: Excellent engine

Head-turning Quotient: A ho-hummer

Ride, Acceleration, Handling: One of the best-handling mid-sized cars in the U.S.

Brakes: Excellent

Suggested Retail Price: Around $20,000

Mileage: About 24 MPG

U.S. Content: 70 - 90%

Mechanically, it's a splendid automobile, a road-runner supreme.

Also, there is the matter of the coffin handles in the Regal Gran Sport's interior door panels. These handles — miniature versions of the type of hand lifts routinely found on caskets — can neither lock nor open the Gran Sport's doors. Why are they there?

All of this nuttiness would be acceptable in a car that was at least consistently bad. The Regal Gran Sport is not. Mechanically, it's a splendid automobile, a road-runner supreme. Geez! It drives me wacko!

Background: The Buick Regal Gran Sport is one of General Motors Corp.'s mid-size, front-wheel-drive, five-passenger family cars — the corporation's "W" class — a lineup that includes the Chevrolet Lumina, Oldsmobile Cutlass Supreme and Pontiac Grand Prix. Of the four, the Chevrolet Lumina is my favorite, because it's the most consistent in design intent — a solid, comfortable, bread-and-butter family car that doesn't pretend to be anything other than what it is.

For 1994, the Lumina, Cutlass Supreme and Grand Prix all come with improved standard, electronically fuel-injected, 3.1-liter engines rated 160 horsepower at 5,200 rpm with a maximum torque of 185 foot-pounds at 4,000 rpm. That's 20 more horsepower than the 1993-model 3.1-liter V-6.

However, the 1994 Buick Regal Gran Sport keeps its standard 3.8-liter V-6 — a bigger, smoother engine rated 170 horsepower at 4,800 rpm with a maximum torque of 225 foot-pounds at 3,200 rpm.

The Buick Regal is offered as a coupe or sedan in three versions: the base Custom, the upscale Limited and the sporty Gran Sport. The 3.1-liter V-6 is standard on the Regal Limited and Custom. The 3.8-liter V-6 is available as an option on those cars.

Complaints: One of my biggest gripes about the tested 1993 Regal Gran Sport was that it lacked an air bag, an unforgivable omission for a car in its class. Happily, that matter has been taken care of for 1994. A driver's air bag is standard in the new Regal, as it is in the 1994 Oldsmobile Cutlass Supreme and Pontiac Grand Prix.

Praise: GM's 3.8-liter V-6 is an excellent engine that has been pushed close to superior for 1993 and 1994. The updated engine is quieter and a bit more fuel efficient, by about one mile per gallon, than is its predecessor. Praise also goes to the standard anti-lock, power four-wheel-disc brakes on the Regal Gran Sport. Thumbs up to overall body construction, which is excellent.

Head-turning quotients:
• Regal Gran Sport sedan — head-scratching ho-hummer.
• Chevrolet Lumina sedan — boxy butt, sexy front.
• Oldsmobile Cutlass Supreme sedan — very definitely your father's Oldsmobile.
• Pontiac Grand Prix sedan — too sexy for your daddy, too sexy for your mama, on the leading edge of Middle American libido.

Ride, acceleration and handling: The Regal Gran Sport, outfitted with 16-inch Goodyear Eagle tires and a front-strut, rear multi-link suspension, is one of the best-handling mid-size cars available in the U.S. market. Similarly outfitted Lumina, Cutlass Supreme and Grand Prix models also ride and handle well.

Mileage: As noted in the 1993 Regal Gran Sport with the 3.8-liter V-6, about 24 to the gallon (16.5-gallon tank, estimated 380-mile range on usable volume of regular unleaded), combined city-highway, running with one to four occupants and light cargo.

The Gran Sport was equipped with a standard, four-speed automatic transmission. For 1993, a three-speed automatic transmission was standard in the Lumina, Cutlass Supreme and Grand Prix base cars; but four-speed automatics were available in upgraded versions of those cars.

Sound system: As found in the 1993 Regal Gran Sport, AM/FM stereo radio and compact disc by GM/Delco. No cassette, which should've been included. Outstanding sound all around. (In driving hundreds of GM cars and trucks, I have rarely found a bad sound system.)

Price note: Even with the aggressive streamlining of its product lines, begun in 1992, GM continues to offer myriad option packages for its cars and trucks. Those options can boost prices. This certainly is true of the corporation's "W" models.

Still, in 1994, it's possible to pick up a well-equipped GM "W" car for under $20,000. Comparison shop these models for the best price. Keep in mind that they are essentially the same cars, built on the same platform. Differences, such as they exist, primarily are in styling.

Coming changes: Besides the improved 3.1-liter V-6 engine and the installation of standard driver's air bags, GM's 1994 mid-size cars also get standard power door locks and Pass-Key II theft-deterrent systems. A two-tone, exterior paint job will be standard on 1994 Buick Regal Gran Sport models. But the biggest changes in GM's mid-size car lineup will come in the 1995-model year and several model years beyond.

A redesigned Chevrolet Lumina sedan, devoid of any boxiness, will appear in early 1994 as a 1995 model. The car will have two front air bags — one for the driver and one for the front-seat passenger. An upgraded version of GM's 3.8-liter V-6 will go into the new Lumina, along with a four-speed automatic transmission.

GM's Chevrolet division eventually will drop the Lumina name in favor of a revival of the Monte Carlo moniker, which will appear first on a 1995 Chevy coupe.

More radical revisions of the "W" cars will occur with remakes of the Buick Regal, Pontiac Grand Prix and Oldsmobile Cutlass Supreme. As has happened in previous revampings of its car lines, introductions of GM's new "W" class will take place on a staggered basis. The Chevrolet Lumina/Monte Carlo is scheduled to be the first out of the box.

Hometowns: The Buick Regal and Chevrolet Lumina are built in Oshawa, Ontario. The Pontiac Grand Prix is assembled in Fairfax, Kan. The Oldsmobile Cutlass Supreme is assembled in Doraville, Ga.

EAGLE Vision TSi

EAGLE Vision TSi

Praise: Superior overall design

Head-turning Quotient: Hot *and* practical

Ride, Acceleration, Handling: Top marks, all around

Suggested Retail Price: $21,404

Mileage: About 23 MPG

U.S. Content: 72%

With Notes on the Chrysler Concorde and Dodge Intrepid

Chrysler Corp. is the Easter company. It's been dead and resurrected so many times, it ought to have a place on the liturgical calendar.

I mean no religious disrespect. This revelation came to me in a vision, an Eagle Vision TSi, one of Chrysler's splendiferous new LH platform cars.

The Vision TSi made me believe. Yes! Turned me away from the crooked path of doubt and cynicism. Glory! It made me believe that Chrysler — once the prodigal child of the U.S. auto industry, once an unrepentant sinner in matters of design and quality, once a company that showed all of the signs of being headed toward corporate perdition — it made me believe that Chrysler will live!

It's a miracle! But, hey, don't take it on faith. I mean, we're talking business, here. You pay good money for a family passenger car. You want and deserve a good product. That's understood.

So, what you've got to do is go see for yourself. You've got to sit in a Vision TSi, touch it and drive it. You've got to compare it with every other respectable, four-door, five-passenger, front-wheel-drive, mid-size car out there before you hand over your hard-earned cash.

But, yeah, I'm convinced that after you've done all of these things, you will see the light. And even if you don't buy the Vision TSi, you'll understand the distance that Chrysler has traveled from ruination to salvation and say, "Job well done." Hallelujah!

Background: The Eagle Vision and the practically identical Chrysler Concorde and Dodge Intrepid, introduced in 1993, are Chrysler's newest and best-ever mid-size passenger cars. They made everybody's "best" car list in 1993, and they're likely to repeat in 1994.

It's the kind of thing that happens when high-quality and high-content come together with — for the time being, at least — reasonable prices.

Check out the content: All LH cars have standard dual-front air bags. Power four-wheel-disc brakes with anti-lock backup are standard on the Eagle Vision TSi, Chrysler Concorde, and Dodge Intrepid ES. The anti-lock

Eagle Vision TSi

system is optional on other LH cars. Optional built-in child-safety seats are available on all LH models.

Other standard equipment on the Vision TSi includes an automatic air conditioner and fog lights.

Personal choice: My favorite LH is the Vision TSi, which comes with a standard 3.5-liter, 24-valve, electronically fuel injected V-6 rated 214 horsepower at 5,800 rpm, with a maximum torque of 221 foot-pounds at 2,800 rpm. The standard engine for the base LH cars is a 3.3-liter V-6 rated 153 horsepower at 5,300 rpm, with a maximum torque of 177 horsepower at 2,800 rpm.

Also standard on the TSi is Chrysler's second-level, "touring" suspension, which gets to do its curve-handling thing in conjunction with grippy, sticky 16-inch tires.

In all, there are three suspensions — base, "touring," and "performance" — available in the LH car line. All three are good, but buyers should be aware that the "performance" suspension is substantially more jarring than the others.

Complaints: Some people who took turns at the wheel of the Vision TSi complained that the car's engine was too noisy. Others said that, for a sporty car, the Vision TSi's exhaust note was not loud enough. Everyone criticized the absence of an illuminated indicator on the floor-mounted, gearshift console. They were not placated by Chrysler's decision to place a second shift indicator, this one lighted, in the lower right-hand corner of the speedometer. I agree. A simple, illuminated, floor-mounted console indicator would've been enough.

Praise: Superior overall design, engineering and construction in a family sedan. The Vision TSi is super-tight, which gives it the feel of an expensive sports coupe — a feeling that belies the car's humongous interior.

Indeed, there's enough space in the Vision TSi's cabin to establish demilitarized zones for warring passengers. If push comes to shove, really ornery types can be shoved into car's big trunk, which has 22.5 cubic feet of cargo space.

Head-turning quotients:
- Eagle Vision TSi — a passionate marriage, styling that combines the hot with the practical.
- Chrysler Concorde — what love must be like among the rich and famous: elegant, somewhat restrained, but quite enjoyable.
- Dodge Intrepid — open shirt, hairy chest and gold chain, and maybe a cigar; obvious in seductive intent, a stylistic come-on with performance to match persona.

Ride, acceleration and handling: Top marks all around, though some passengers said the Vision TSi's "touring" suspension was a bit hard. Had they sat upon the optional, sports-car-hard "performance" suspension, they would've really had something to complain about. As tested, the Vision TSi was a hoot!

Mileage: As noted in the Vision TSi with the 3.5-liter engine, about 23 miles per gallon (18-gallon tank, estimated 400-mile range on usable volume of recommended premium unleaded), running mostly highway with one to five occupants and light cargo.

Sound system: In the tested Vision TSi, optional 11-speaker, AM/FM stereo radio and cassette with compact disc. Chrysler/Infinity system. Excellent.

Price note: Chrysler boosted the price of its LH cars by $100 in January 1993 and by another $200 in April of that year. Toward the end of the 1993-model year, the Eagle Vision TSi was selling for $21,404 with a dealer's invoice of $18,743; the Chrysler Concorde, $18,641 with a dealer's invoice of $16,365; and the Dodge Intrepid ES, $17,489, with a dealer's invoice of $15,371. Both the base Dodge and Eagle LH cars were selling for under $18,000.

Assuming continued strong demand for the LH cars, I expect more price increases on these models in 1994.

Coming changes: Lots of very fine tuning for 1994. That includes a more powerful, standard 3.3-liter V-6 engine, recalibrated to run 161 horsepower at 5,300 rpm, with a maximum torque of 181 foot-pounds at 3,200 rpm. A flexible-fuel version of that engine, using 85-percent methanol alcohol and 15-percent gasoline (M85) will be available. The M85 engine is rated 167 horsepower at 5,400 rpm with a maximum torque of 185 foot-pounds at 3,000 rpm.

Other 1994 changes in Chrysler's LH lineup include an improved four-speed automatic transmission and improved noise, vibration and harshness control.

Hometown: Chrysler's LH cars are built in Bramalea, Ontario. Some LH production will be moved to Newark, Del. in 1994.

FORD Taurus SHO

I will never again say nasty things to people in traffic. I will never again lift my hand in Ignoble Salute to people who cut in front of me, or who engage in other impolite behavior behind the wheel. I have learned my lesson. I am humbled.

It happened this way:

I was driving along the District of Columbia's weekday streets at about 6 p.m. I was tired and rushed. My mood was foul.

Along came a brother in what appeared to be a late-model Corvette. I was driving a midnight blue, 1993 Ford Taurus SHO, a hot-rod in humble clothing. The dude in the Corvette was tailgating me.

I moved to the right lane to give the Corvette driver space. He pulled alongside of me, honking his horn. I was, ah, ticked off. I lowered my window and shouted: "Yo mama!"

There is a moment after you've done something stupid when you know you've done something irretrievably, irrevocably stupid. It is an embarrassing, still point that drains the blood from your *soul.*

I was at that point.

My mind raced.

"Oh, no!" I thought. "What if that dude works for the *Washington Post?* What if he's a reader? What if he has a gun?"

I shouted again: "Yamaha! Yamaha! It has a Yamaha engine!"

The brother looked at me, puzzled. He smiled.

"That's the new automatic SHO?" he asked.

Praise: A dynamite runner

Head-turning Quotient: Sneaky passion

Ride, Acceleration, Handling: Excellent

Brakes: Excellent

Suggested Retail Price: $24,829

Mileage: About 23 MPG

U.S. Content: 85%

Ford Taurus SHO

One of the hottest

automatic-

transmission cars

available.

"Sho is," I said, and thanked God that I sometimes mispronounce the simplest of words.

Background: Ford Motor Co. did a major rework of its Taurus cars in 1992, streamlining the bodies of the now-famous mid-size family sedans and ditching the base model, the Taurus L. Those changes helped the front-wheel-drive Taurus scoot ahead of the Honda Accord in passenger car sales. But if you looked closely at the numbers, you would've found that the best of the Taurus cars, the powerful SHO (Special High Output), was lagging on the sales charts.

It seems that Americans like the idea of high-performance cars; but *they don't like using the five-speed manual sticks traditionally found in such models.* That was the problem with the SHO, which initially was sold only with a manual gearbox.

For 1993, and 1994, the SHO can be ordered with an optional, four-speed automatic transmission, such as that found in the test car.

The new automatic transmission is linked to a larger Yamaha engine, a 3.2-liter, 24-valve V-6 rated 220 horsepower at 6,000 rpm, with a maximum torque of 215 foot-pounds at 4,800 rpm. The standard transmission remains a five-speed manual linked to a 3-liter, 24-valve Yamaha V-6 rated 220 horsepower at 6,200 rpm, with a maximum torque of 200 foot-pounds at 4,800 rpm.

Complaints: The automatic SHO sometimes feels as if it's going to leave you standing, even though you're hanging onto the wheel. But the sensation is more "feel" than real. You eventually get used to this car and learn to control it.

Praise: A dynamite runner. Faster than all get-out. One of the hottest automatic-transmission cars available. And the fun of it is that SHO looks so respectable, so Mom and Pop, with the exceptions of a rear decklid spoiler and a set of fancy, "sparkle spoke" cast aluminum wheels.

Dual-front air bags are standard in all Taurus cars for 1994. The SHO also comes with standard power four-wheel disc brakes — with larger rotors and calipers for 1994 — and a standard anti-lock brake system.

Head-turning quotient: A splendid work of sneaky passion. Folks see it and don't see it. But if you're behind the wheel, you sure as heck feel it.

Ride, acceleration, handling: Excellent ride and acceleration. Handling is great, once you get used to the automatic SHO's lightning starts. Braking is excellent.

Mileage: About 23 to the gallon (18.4-gallon tank, estimated 413-mile range on usable volume of regular unleaded), combined city-highway, mostly driver only.

Coming changes: In addition to the dual-front bags and improved disc brakes shared by other 1994 Taurus models, SHO models equipped with manual transmissions get new speed-rated tires designed to better dissipate heat and prolong wear.

Sound system: AM/FM stereo radio and cassette with compact disc, optional Ford JBL Audio System. Totally boss.

Price: Yo, mama! Base price is $24,829. Dealer invoice is $21,245. Price as tested is $26,761, including $1,407 in options and a $525 destination charge. Purse-strings note: If you want a decent family car, buy a regular Taurus, a reasonably well-equipped GL sedan that starts at $15,600. If you want to SHO off without sweating, go for the automatic SHO.

FORD Taurus LX Wagon

With Notes on the Mercury Sable Wagon

I had avoided normalcy because of its proximity to boredom. But you can't run away from things forever. The Taurus LX wagon was on the test-drive schedule. There were things and people that had to be moved. Cir-

Ford Taurus LX wagon

Praise: Best large station wagon available

Head-turning Quotient: Spins heads

Ride, Acceleration, Handling: I like, I like…

Brakes: Excellent

Suggested Retail Price: $20,100

Mileage: About 24 MPG

U.S. Content: 90%

cumstance and obligation came together. I took the wagon. I'm glad I did.

But, first, a definition.

Automotive "normalcy" means affordable and practical. That usually means what car marketers call a "family vehicle" — a term they use with all of the enthusiasm of a Times Square theater promoting a G-rated movie.

The Taurus LX wagon *is* a family vehicle. But there's not much normal about it. Take handling, for example. Station wagons often wiggle-waggle around curves, particularly if the curves are taken at speed. The Taurus LX wagon snuggles instead of wiggles. It burrows deep into the turn and stays there — with little perceptible yaw.

The Taurus LX wagon does this consistently. I know. I've driven several of those wagons since 1990. With one exception, they behaved as admirably as the tested 1993 model, even under load.

Aesthetically, the "norm" for large station wagons has been ugliness — big, square, lumbering ugliness. That is not the case with the Taurus LX. This smooth, rounded, front-wheel-drive wagon has always been a good-looker. Subtle exterior and interior changes in 1992 made it look even better.

Still, I could do without the lower-body cladding on the Taurus LX. But, hey, lots of people want that stuff. They think it looks good. They think it separates their Taurus wagon from normal Taurus wagons that have no cladding. See what I mean? It ain't normal to be normal.

Background: The Taurus wagon and sedan and their mechanically identical Mercury Sable stable mates were introduced as 1986 models and spiffed up in 1992, the year when the Taurus aced out the Honda Accord as the best-selling car in the United States.

Taurus sales remained strong in 1993, albeit with the help of rebates. But the criticism that people have been buying those cars because Ford's been "giving them away" is a bum rap. Most people aren't stupid. You can't sell them trash with discounts.

The Taurus/Sable wagons are good, period. They have gargantuan cargo capacity — 81.1 cubic feet with the middle seats down, 47.5 cubic feet with the middle seats up. *For 1994, dual-front air bags are standard, as are 15-inch tires and wheels. Both models can be equipped with optional tailgate picnic tables, which come in handy at freeway rest stops and tailgate parties.*

The Taurus wagon is available as a standard GL and upscale LX model. The Sable wagon is available as a standard GS and upscale LS.

The standard engine in the Taurus/Sable wagons is a 3-liter V-6 rated 140 horsepower at 4,800 rpm with a maximum torque of 160 foot-pounds at 3,000 rpm. The Taurus LX wagon gets a standard 3.8-liter V-6 rated 140 horsepower at 3,800 rpm with a maximum torque of 215 foot-pounds at 2,200 rpm. The higher-torque, 3.8-liter engine is available as an option for the Sable wagon.

Complaints: Occasional glitches in fit-and-finish, usually around the dashboard, found in Taurus/Sable wagons driven in the 1991 and 1992-model years. The 1993 Taurus LX was tight and right.

A Taurus LX wagon I tested in 1990 sometimes, inexplicably, cut off right after ignition. It was the only time that problem occurred in four years of driving Taurus/Sable wagons and sedans.

Praise: The Taurus/Sable wagons are the best large station wagons available in terms of overall design, content, cost, quality and safety, performance and cost. Had I needed a wagon for other than occasional use, the Taurus LX would've been tops on my shopping list

Head-turning quotient:

• Taurus LX wagon — spins many heads atop blue, pink, and white collars.

• Mercury Sable LS — the Grey Poupon of station wagons, suburbs with attitude, about as far as you can go with this automotive genre without engaging in ostentatious display.

Ride, acceleration and handling: I like. I like. I like. Braking is excellent. The tested 1993 Taurus LX wagon was equipped with optional power four-wheel discs with anti-lock backup. Standard brakes on both Taurus and Sable wagons include front discs/rear drums.

Mileage: As noted in the 1993 Taurus LX, about 24 to the gallon (16-gallon tank, estimated 374-mile range on usable volume of regular unleaded), combined city-highway, carrying up to five occupants and 325 pounds of cargo.

An electronically controlled, four-speed automatic transmission is standard in the Taurus and Sable wagons.

Sound system: In the 1993 Taurus LX, 80-watt AM/FM stereo radio and cassette. Optional Ford High-Level Audio System. Pretty darned good.

Price note: Toward the end of the 1993-model years, the Taurus LX had a suggested retail price of $20,100 with a dealer's invoice of $17,225. The comparable Mercury Sable LS (with the standard 3-liter V-6) was priced at $19,750 with dealer's invoice of $16,780. Ford most likely will hold the line on these prices in 1994. Price increases, if any, probably will be modest and offset by rebates.

Coming changes: Other 1994 Taurus changes include ozone-friendly R-134A air conditioner regrigerant, color-keyed handles on all models, "crystalin" (clear) headlamps, and bright machined wheels on the LX.

But keep in mind that Ford is completely redoing its Taurus platform for the 1995 model year. The new Taurus cars will have a lower, more steeply sloped hoodline. Also, the 1995 Taurus models will be shorter than the current Taurus cars, but will have a longer wheelbase — the centerline distance between front and rear wheels.

This means that Ford is going after the Chrysler LH car franchise with designs that push the front and rear wheels to the farthest extremities of the car in bid to create more interior space.

The likelihood is that those and other changes, under wraps at this writing, will be reflected in the Mercury Sable line as well.

Hometowns: Ford Taurus/Mercury Sable wagons and cars are assembled in Atlanta, Ga. and Chicago, Ill.

HONDA Accord LX Sedan

The 1994 Honda Accord LX Sedan is a work of uncertain passion, an ode to motorized androgyny. Stylistically, there is nothing about it to hate, little about it to love.

In this regard, the new Accord is not the breakthrough car Honda

Honda Accord LX

wanted it to be — at least, not for me. It's a personal bias. When it comes to Honda Accord styling, I'm left cold. The car's body has never excited me.

Such is the situation with the 1994 model, which has new sheet metal, but still resides in a purgatory absent anything ugly or beautiful. Only the rear end gives some hint of soul. It's more muscular, more sinewy than the 1993 model. It even has a bit of urban funk: the Accord sedan's C-pillars, those framing the rear window, resemble the sail panels on a Cadillac Eldorado. I like that.

The front end is something else. I hate it. It's a celibate face marked by a blandness so pervasive, it gives me chills.

That makes me mad. In terms of interior design and mechanical function, the 1994 Accord LX sedan is a fine, spirited car. Is it too much to ask that Honda give it a body to match?

Background: What Honda omitted in exterior styling, it included in value engineering. The 1994 Honda Accord — the fifth generation of the car since its introduction in 1976 — represents one of the best buys in family cars available.

Just look at the list:

• Dual-front air bags are standard on all 1994 Accord models — sedans, coupes, and wagons. The sedans and coupes have three trim levels — base DX, midline LX, and sport-luxury EX. Wagons are available in LX and EX trim only.

Complaints: Low head-room in the rear seats	
Praise: Superb fit-and-finish	
Head-turning Quotient: Nada	
Ride, Acceleration, Handling: Excellent	
Brakes: Kudos	
Suggested Retail Price: Around $22,000	
Mileage: About 25 MPG	
U.S. Content: 75%	

This is really competitive pricing, meant to appeal to buyers who shop with their heads instead of their hearts.

•All 1994 Accords meet the federal government's 1997 side-impact, crash protection standards.

•Anti-lock brakes with with power four-wheel-disc brakes are standard on the top-line Accord EX sedans and coupes. The anti-lock system is optional on all other Accord models.

•Cruise control is standard on the LX and EX Accords.

•The tested LX sedan also includes air conditioning, power door locks, power windows and mirrors, and an upgraded sound system as standard equipment.

All Accord models are front-engine, front-wheel-drive. Two 2.2-liter, 16-valve, four-cylinder engines are available for the lineup.

DX and LX models run with the standard Accord four-cylinder engine, rated 130-horsepower at 5,300 rpm with a maximum torque of 139 foot-pounds at 4,200 rpm. The EX gets Honda's VTEC four-cylinder engine, rated 145 horsepower at 5,500 rpm with a maximum torque of 147 foot-pounds at 4,500 rpm.

A five-speed manual transmission is standard for all 1994 Accord models. An electronically controlled, four-speed automatic transmission with "grade logic" is available for all versions of the car.

"Grade logic" denotes the transmission computer's ability to automatically select the correct shift points, say, when you're going up or down a hill. This reduces "gear hunting" — often manifested by bothersome, inadvertent downshifting in many four-cylinder cars — when travelling over hilly terrains.

Complaints: Bland exterior styling.

Praise: Overall brilliant engineering, which means you've got to get to know the Accord LX and its siblings to really enjoy them. The trouble for Honda is that there are lots of brilliantly engineered cars in the mid-size car category; and some of them, such as the Nissan Altima, Mitsubishi Galant, and Chrysler Corp.'s splendiferous LH cars, are likable from the moment you see them.

Head-turning quotient: On a 70-mile trek through southern Ohio, no one, not even the police, gave a second look to the 1994 Accord LX. Several journalists driving other 1994 Honda Accords reported the same apparent lack of public response. It could be that folks in Ohio don't get excited about new cars. But the likelihood is that they saw nothing in the new Accord's exterior styling to get excited about.

Ride, acceleration handling: Triple aces. You've *got* to drive the thing to get excited about it. I drove all of the 1994 Accord sedans available, but concentrated on the LX, the one most Americans buy. Some of my fellow gearheads complained about the lack of a six-cylinder engine in the Accord lineup, but they're full of baloney.

With both the optional automatic four-speed and the five-speed manual transmissions, the 130-horsepower LX, on a regulated test track and on the civilian highway, moved with unabashed passion. The 145-horsepower EX was sensational.

Honda can waste time worrying about the lack of a six-cylinder engine if it wants to; but, frankly, I don't see the point.

Braking in the tested LX was excellent. The car was equipped with power assisted, four-wheel disc brakes with anti-lock backup — the optional braking system on the LX. The LX's standard braking system — power-assisted front discs/rear drums — also gets high marks.

Mileage: About 28 to the gallon in the tested LX with five-speed automatic transmission (17-gallon tank, estimated 461-mile range on usable volume of regular unleaded), running mostly rural highway with two occupants; and carrying light cargo (one laptop computer and three travel bags) in the Accord LX's standard 13-fubic-feet trunk.

Sound system: Standard four-speaker, electronically controlled AM/FM stereo radio and cassette, Honda's High-Power Stereo system, excellent.

Price: Here's the really good news: Honda, at least for a while, will hold its 1994 Accord prices at about 1993 levels. That means retail prices will range from $14,300 for the Accord DX sedan to about $22,400 for the EX sedan, with dealer's invoice pricing on the sedans ranging from about $12,000 to $19,000.

This is really competitive pricing, meant to appeal to buyers who shop with their heads instead of their hearts. Here's hoping that Honda dealers stay with the program.

Hometown: The vast majority of Honda Accords sold in the United States are made in the United States by Honda of America Manufacturing in Marysville, Ohio.

MAZDA 626 ES Sedan

I met the car a year ago at an auto show in New York. We exchanged pleasantries and promised to get together; but the vow was devoid of intent.

That was my fault.

My wandering eyes caught other cars, seemingly prettier than the prototype Mazda 626 before me. I was looking at those models, while talking

Mazda 626 ES

to the Mazda. It was the kind of slight that hurts without response from the offended party. Ashamed, I left.

Guilt became avoidance, and I stayed away from the new Mazda 626 for 15 months. That cowardice ended with a phone call. The 1993-model Mazda 626 ES sedan was coming, the man from Mazda said. I waited.

It was an attractive car, dark green with a tan interior. It looked like a small remake of the full-size, luxury Mazda 929 sedan. I said as much to the 626 ES, which, of course, was the wrong thing to do. The car grew sullen. Our first ride was tense.

Things improved on a second and longer trip. The 626 ES was a sedan with sports-car spunk. It wanted to run. I wanted to drive. We went out a lot after that. We parted friends, and promised to stay in touch.

Background: The Mazda 626 has been around since 1979, first appearing as a rear-wheel-drive family sedan and a two-door coupe. The car went front-wheel-drive in 1983, went through more revisions in 1986 and 1988, and was completely redesigned in 1992.

Through all of those changes, the 626's function remained the same — to serve as Mazda's bread-and-butter car, a mid-size, mid-priced people hauler that puts function before form.

Thus, it's no wonder that the current iteration runs on borrowed personality, that of the sumptuous Mazda 929.

The idea is to provide "visual continuity" between the 626 and the 929, say Mazda's marketers, to link the two cars in the minds of consumers, to make it easier for those who buy the 626 to move up to the 929.

It's a risky strategy.

The 626 runs, feels, and looks good enough to keep buyers out of the larger 929 forever. And should an owner decide to leave the 626, that person is apt to look beyond Mazda for a replacement, inasmuch as the 626 and 929 are so similar.

There are three 626 models: the base DX, more upscale LX, and the tested top-of-the-line ES, which is equipped with a 2.5 liter, dual-overhead-cam, 24-valve V6 rated 164 horsepower at 5,600 rpm. Max torque on that engine is 160 foot-pounds at 4,800 rpm.

The DX and LX come with a standard, 2-liter, 16-valve, inline four-cylinder engine rated 118 horsepower at 5,500 rpm and 127 foot-pounds of torque at 4,500 rpm.

Despite their Mazda nameplate, the 626 models are American cars. They are jointly built by Ford and Mazda at the same Michigan plant that assembles Ford Probe and Mazda MX-6 sports coupes.

Complaint: The standard transmission in the 626 sedans is a five-speed manual, which I think is just a slick way of charging people more money for the optional four-speed, electronically controlled automatic transmission. Think about it. Sixty-seven percent of all Mazda 626 cars in the United States are sold with automatic transmissions. Overall, 79 percent of the new cars in this country are sold with automatics. Why not standardize the most popular system and make optional the system that's least popular? Wouldn't that be best for consumers?

Praise: The Mazda 626 is a well-done family car that offers high performance and lots of amenities — despite the "optional" automatic-transmission gimmick — at an almost reasonable price. The tested version, the 626 ES, is motorized vanilla at its best — rich, smooth, enjoyable, but wanting in anything excitingly different.

For 1994, dual-air bags — along with ocone-friendly R-134A air conditioner regrigerant — are standard in all 626 models. Four-wheel disc brakes are standard on the ES, while front discs/rear drums are standard on the DX and LX. Anti-lock brakes are optional on all 626 models.

Head-turning quotient: "Say, aren't you related to the 929?" The 626 ES and LaToya Jackson, singer Michael Jackson's petulant little sister, have lots in common.

Ride, acceleration, handling: Top mid-size car performance in all three categories. The 626 ES seats and rides four adults comfortably. Acceleration requires vigorous gear-shifting in the test car, but the thing

---

Complaints: *Optional* automatic transmission

Praise: Motorized vanilla at its best — rich and smooth

Head-turning Quotient: Aren't you related to the 929?

Ride, Acceleration, Handling: A top performance

Brakes: Excellent

Suggested Retail Price: $18,995

Mileage: About 23 MPG

U.S. Content: 75%

reaches high speeds without groaning or moaning. Braking was excellent. The test model came with the optional anti-lock system.

Sound system: AM/FM stereo radio and cassette, installed by Mazda. Optional compact disc player installed by dealer. System not good in test car — disc player skipped, tape player sped up. But identical system in another 1993 Mazda 626 worked perfectly.

Mileage: Approximately 23 to the gallon (15.5-gallon tank, estimated 335-mile range on usable volume of recommended premium unleaded gasoline), running mostly highway and driver only.

Price note: Toward the end of the 1993-model year, the 626 ES had a base price of $18,995 and a dealer's invoice of $16,540. The car's quality has always been much better than its sales, which means that Mazda may try to hold the line on pricing in 1994 to help improve the 626's market chances.

Hometown: The Mazda 626 is assembled by AutoAlliance International Inc., the Ford-Mazda joint venture, in Flat Rock, Mich.

Complaints: Road and wind noise

Praise: A must-shop car

Head-turning Quotient: What's that bulge on the hood?

Ride, Acceleration, Handling: Excellent, but a bit soft

Brakes: Excellent

Suggested Retail Price: $20,000

Mileage: About 27 MPG

U.S. Content: 60%

MITSUBISHI Galant GS

It was white with a gray velour interior — totally Ozzie-and-Harriet in terms of automotive fabric and color. It was the 1994 Mitsubishi Galant GS, and it looked middle-class and married with children — until you examined its details.

There was, for example, a bulge on the left side of the Galant GS' sleek, low hood. Mitsubishi's designers added that touch to accommodate the geometry of the car's double-overhead cam engine, while preserving the overall slope of the car's front end.

To me, the "cam bulge" looked like a snake's nostril. But a Virginia friend saw things differently.

"I haven't seen anything like that since my last high-school dance," she said.

"Hunh?" I asked.

"High school. Slow dancing. You know. That hood looks like a boy who's been dancing too close."

She really said that.

I looked at her with amazement. It was the first time she'd ever said anything like that to me. Hell, I never knew she slow-danced.

Mitsubishi Galant GS

I took a second look at the Galant GS. Snake nostril, or whatever, it just didn't look like a family car anymore.

Background: Since its introduction in the late 1980s the Mitsubishi Galant has had trouble defining itself. Family car or "sports sedan"? Mom and pop, or "Henry and June"? Things were in a muddle.

So, Mitsubishi's leaders went back to the marketplace and asked people to rank their needs and wants for a new mid-size car. Reliability, quality, durability and safety got top marks. Turbochargers, intercoolers, garish plastic air dams and 0-to-60 times got the boot. That meant throwing out high-performance models, such as the Galant GSR and VR4.

The result is a new Galant that's long on sizzle, but short on flash. This car has lots of standard adult stuff — dual-side air bags, environmentally friendly air conditioner refrigerant, high-tensile steel tubular door beams (instead of the usual pressed-steel variety used by many auto makers for side-impact protection), anti-flammable upholstery, and height-adjustable front shoulder belts. A very respectable car.

But, again, there's that bulge. In three Galant models — the base S, slightly less-base ES, and upscale LS — the bulge helps cover up a single-overhead cam, 2.4-liter, four-cylinder, 16-valve engine rated 141 horsepower at 5,500 rpm with a maximum torque of 148 foot-pounds at 3,000 rpm.

In the sporty GS, the bulge covers a double-overhead cam version of

Mom and Pop, or

"Henry and June"?

that engine rated 160 horsepower at 6,000 rpm with a maximum torque of 160 foot-pounds at 4,250 rpm.

No V-6 is available for the 1994 Galant models.

A five-speed manual transmission is standard on the S and GS. A four-speed, electronically controlled automatic transmission (with "fuzzy logic" to help reduce downshifting) is standard on the ES and LS and optional on the S and GS.

Anti-lock brakes are optional on the ES, LS, and GS; they are not available on the S.

All Galants are front-wheel-drive, five-seat sedans.

Complaints: The new Galant is substantially tighter and more rigid than its predecessors. That's the good news. The bad news is that the car's stronger body seems to do a better job of transmitting road noise. Wind noise at highway speeds could be reduced, too.

Also, who was the turkey who designed the cup holders to fit right underneath the compact disc? Ejecting a disc with filled cups in the holders can be an interesting and messy experience. How about redesigning this part, Mitsubishi?

Praise: The 1994 Galant GS is competitive with *everything* in the mid-size, family sedan category, even without a V-6. This is a *must-shop* car. Other standard equipment includes an air conditioner and power windows and locks in the ES, LS and GS.

Also, the Galant GS comes with a real trunk — 12.5-cubic feet. That includes a compartment to conceal valuables beneath the trunk floor. Rear seatbacks can be folded down to carry long items, such as skis or hockey sticks.

Head-turning quotient: That bulge attracted lots of attention. Seems like everybody wanted to know why it was there.

Ride, acceleration, handling: Excellent ride and acceleration. Handling felt as if the compromise between passion and practicality went too far. The tested Galant GS was a bit soft in curves.

Braking was excellent. Test car was equipped with the anti-lock option. Power four-wheel disc brakes are standard on the GS. On the other Galant cars, standard brakes are ventilated power front discs/rear drums.

Mileage: About 27 to the gallon (16.9-gallon tank, estimated 444-mile range on usable volume of 89-octane unleaded), running mostly highway and driver only.

Sound system: In the tested Galant GS, a standard six-speaker, AM/FM stereo radio and cassette with compact disc, by Mitsubishi. A good boomer for rock stuff; but a tad off-rhythm in the tape/disc reproduction of jazz and classical music.

Price note: Mitsubishi introduced its 1994 Galants in the spring of 1993. At that time, the tested GS had an estimated price of $20,000. Estimated prices for the lower Galants ranged from near $14,000 to $18,000.

As noted elsewhere in this book, prices on Japanese-nameplate cars have been rising. But Mitsubishi has a chance to steal substantial market share from Toyota, Honda, and the native U.S. Big Three car companies with its revised Galant. Here's betting that Mitsubishi will sacrifice big price hikes in pursuit of a bigger piece of the U.S. mid-size car market.

Hometown: The Mitsubishi Galant is made in Normal, Ill., by Diamond-Star Motors, a joint-venture company formed by Mitsubishi and Chrysler Corp.

NISSAN Altima Sedan

Feeling down? Think you'll never amount to anything? Take heart, and take a spin in the 1993 Nissan Altima sedan. It's proof that failure isn't forever.

The all-new Altima replaced the Stanza as Nissan's mid-size family sedan in 1993. That is, it sort of replaced the Stanza.

The qualifier is needed because Nissan kept the Stanza name, in teeny-tiny letters, on the back of the Altima sedan and the front of the car's user's manual.

Seems as though the only good thing about the Stanza was that it had a good insurance rating, largely because of its claims experience, which meant that the people who bought it tended to be accident-free. By tying the Stanza name to the Altima sedan, Nissan retained a favorable insurance rating for its new car, although the new model is quite different from its predecessor. And you thought these things were done with common sense. Ha!

But, anyway, we're talking about success, which the Altima represents in Nissan's long-running, but heretofore fruitless effort to find a comfortable spot in the market for mid-size family sedans. The Stanza, introduced in 1982, just couldn't cut it in that segment. It was an ugly car bereft of personality. Even thieves hated the thing, which also helped to improve its insurance rating.

The Altima, on the other hand, is a far superior automobile, a work of rounded elegance that pays homage to practicality without embracing boredom. It's a cuddly car, a four-wheeled bug. Makes you feel good just to sit in it.

Complaints: Automatic front seat belts

Praise: A solid family sedan

Head-turning Quotient: Yo!

Ride, Acceleration, Handling: Triple "Yo!" One of the smoothest, most-balanced rides available

Brakes: Good

Suggested Retail Price: $18,549

Mileage: About 25 MPG

U.S. Content: 60%

Nissan Altima Sedan

Drawbacks? Yeah. In its first year on the market, the Altima picked up lots of young buyers — the hip and the flip, people who have a zest for life and a lust for risk. Car thieves, who have a knack for emulation, started paying attention to the Altima, too. The Altima is still hanging onto its favorable "average" insurance rating; but you can bet your boopies that insurers are paying close attention to the accident/theft claims experience of the car. Here's betting that, in another year or two, the insurers will jack up the premiums on that car.

Background: The Altima's strategy for taking a hunk out of the mid-size car market is simple: Give buyers an attractive, affordable family sedan that looks and feels more expensive than it is. It's a variation of the fake-fur routine. Who gives a hoot if the fur is phony as long as it looks real, keeps you warm and wears well? Judging from the public's reaction to the tested 1993 Altima GLE sedan, that approach should work wonders for Nissan's bottom line.

All Altimas are front-wheel-drive, five-passenger cars. Models include the base XE, sporty SE, upscale GXE, and top-line GLE.

Complaints: Under federal law (effective September 1, 1993), cars must have full-front passive restraints — dual-front air bags, or automatically closing seat belts. Consumers generally hate the automatic belts. They want bags. But many auto makers, for a variety of reasons, will not be able to supply dual-front bags until 1996 — two years before federal law requires dual-front bags to be placed in *all* new cars sold in the United States.

In the interim, to make do — to placate customers on one hand while complying with current federal law on the other — a number of auto makers are providing driver's air bags in conjunction with automatic front seat belts. This is what Nissan has done in the Altima. Yecchh!

Just remember that those goofy automatic belts are not fully automatic. Only the shoulder harnesses are automatic. You and your front-seat passenger must latch the *manual* lap belt to get full belt protection.

Also, remember this: Air bags — driver's-side or dual-front — are *supplemental crash protection devices*. They must be used with seat belts, regardless of whether those seat belts are manual or "automatic."

Praise: The Altima is an overall excellent rework of the dismal Stanza. What we're talking about in the Altima is a solid, well-presented family sedan. In all of its versions, the car has a decent amount of standard equipment. The GLE has the most standard good stuff, including a four-speed automatic transmission, compact disc player, power sunroof, and a head-up display that projects the speed and other information onto the windshield.

Anti-lock brakes and traction control are available as optional equipment.

Head-turning quotient: Gets a "Yo!"

Ride, acceleration and handling: Triple "Yo!" A four-wheel independent suspension system, with rear struts mounted to subframes front and rear, is standard in all Altima models. Upshot? One of the smoothest, most-balanced rides available in any mid-size car.

Engine work in the Altima GLE is more than adequate. Credit one of the most powerful four-cylinder boomers on the market — a 2.4-liter, double-overhead cam, 16-valve job rated 150 horsepower at 5,600 rpm with a maximum torque of 154 foot-pounds at 4,400 rpm.

Braking is good. Standard brakes in the GLE, GXE and XE include power front disc/rear drums. Power four-wheel discs are standard on the SE.

Mileage: As noted in the tested Altima GLE, about 25 miles per gallon (15.9-gallon tank, estimated 380-mile range on usable volume of regular unleaded), combined city-highway, running with one to four occupants and light cargo.

Sound system: Six-speaker AM/FM stereo radio, cassette and compact disc in the GLE. Installed by Nissan. Excellent.

Price note: The GLE, the most expensive car in the Altima line, had a manufacturers suggested retail price of $18,549 toward the end of the 1993-model year. The dealer's invoice was $16,082. The Altima is a high-demand car, which means its prices probably will rise a bit in 1994. Still, in

The Altima is an overall excellent rework of the dismal Stanza. A solid, well-presented family sedan. One of the smoothest, most-balanced rides available in any mid-size car.

the new year, it will be possible to get a reasonably well-equipped Altima for under $15,000.

Coming changes: Fine tuning. Nothing major in 1994.

Hometown: The Nissan Altima is assembled in Smyrna, Tenn.

Complaints: "Achieva"?! What the heck is that? No air bags

Praise: Overall excellent quality. Standard anti-lock brakes

Head-turning Quotient: Nothing much

Ride, Acceleration, Handling: All excellent

Suggested Retail Price: $13,049

Mileage: About 26 MPG

U.S. Content: 90%

OLDSMOBILE Achieva SC

With Notes on the Pontiac Grand Am and Buick Skylark

The Oldsmobile Achieva is a perfect example of how General Motors can take a good idea and overdo it to the point of befuddlement.

The car's very name exemplifies the problem: "Achieva." What the heck is that? A rap-song pronunciation of "achiever"? A misspelled word on a fifth-grade vocabulary test? A code? None of the above?

Oldsmobile's publicists said the name comes from "advanced research efforts" — big-time marketing studies. In the research, the Achieva name "hit the intended mark by communicating a compact, dependable, nimble and responsible automobile," the publicists said.

Oh, gag me with a survey! They had to do studies to come up with a name like that? What are they, a bunch of "overachievas"?

Other examples of overreaching abound in this car. Look at the Achieva's array of engines. There are four — *four* different engines for one line of compact cars from one division within a company that sells two other practically identical cars under different names!

That kind of product mix can turn car shopping into an SAT exam; and that's bound to turn off some tight-fisted underachievers who simply want to buy a car without having to worry about whether they guessed right or wrong on the bottom line.

Background: The Achieva, introduced in 1992, replaced the Cutlass Calais in Oldsmobile's "lower" mid-size car line. The Achieva runs with — or against, depending on your perspective — the mechanically and dimensionally identical Pontiac Grand Am and Buick Skylark.

Only styling differentiates those cars; and the Pontiac Grand Am, one of Pontiac's best sellers, has the hottest styling.

There are five Achieva cars — the S Coupe (SC) two-door, the S four-door sedan, the upscale SL Coupe (SLC), the SL four-door, and the hot-to-trot Achieva SCX (sports coupe extra).

The Achieva's four available engines include the base, eight-valve, 2.3-liter, inline four-cylinder Quad Overhead Cam (OHC) rated 115 horsepower

Oldsmobile Achieva SL

at 5,200 rpm with a maximum torque of 140 foot-pounds at 3,200 rpm; a 16-valve Quad 4 rated 155 horsepower at 6,000 rpm with a maximum torque of 150 foot-pounds at 4,800 rpm; a "high-output" version of the Quad 4 rated 1185 horsepower at 6,800 rpm with a maximum torque of 160 foot-pounds at 5,200 rpm; and, whew! — a new-for-1994 3.1-liter V-g rated 160 horsepower at 5,200 rpm with a maximum torque of 185 foot-pounds at 2,000 rpm.

The Pontiac Grand Am and Buick Skylark also share the base Quad 4 engine and the 3.1-liter V-6. A few other engines are available for the Grand AM; but, whoa! We'd all go nuts with the details.

Complaints: Too much! Egads! I drove the Achieva SC in 1992 and 1993, both with the high-output Quad 4 engines mated to a standard five-speed manual transmission. Those cars are great fun, their name notwithstanding. I also took a short run in a 115-horsepower Achieva S sedan with a three-speed automatic transmission. That under-Achieva was a total failure in the fun-to-drive department.

Why, oh why can't GM give us one or, at most, two Achieva cars that work the way an Achieva is supposed to work?

Praise: Overall quality and design of the Achieva SC is excellent. The car felt good, although there was a bit too much power in its power steering, which made the steering feel light.

Anti-lock brakes are standard on the Achieva, Grand Am, and Skylark.

Overall quality and design of the Achieva SC is excellent.

73

Head-turning quotients:
• Achieva SC — all of the appeal of a Brooks Brothers suit bought at discount.
• Buick Skylark — wild thangg! Totally, totally wacko with its pointy nose and a mammary-styled dashboard that resembles Madonna in repose.
• Pontiac Grand Am — a splendid work of acceptable passion.

Ride, acceleration and handling: All excellent in the tested Achieva SC models. All pretty lousy — with the happy exception of braking — in the base Achieva S sedan.

Mileage: In the 1993 Achieva SC, about 26 to the gallon (15.2-gallon tank, estimated 385-mile range on usable volume of regular unleaded), running mostly highway and driver only, no cargo.

Sound system: In the 1993 Achieva SC, six-speaker AM/FM stereo radio and cassette by GM/Delco. Very nice boogie.

Coming changes: For 1994, the Achieva line gets a four-door model, the SL sports sedan. The new car will be outfitted with a touring suspension package, 16-inch tires on alloy wheels, dual exhaust pipes, fog lamps, rear aero wing, and a leather-wrapped steering wheel and shifter. But, most of all, the Achieva SL and the rest of its siblings will come with a standard driver's air bag, which is something those cars should've had all along.

Other changes include ozone-friendly R-134A air conditioner refrigerant and a battery-rundown protection system.

Price note: Toward the end of the 1993-model year, the Achieva SC had a base price of $13,049 with a dealer's invoice of $11,809. GM is fighting to build market share, which means that it will keep the lid on Achieva prices in 1994. You should be able to get a reasonably equipped Achieva for under $15,000.

Hometown: The Oldsmobile Achieva, Pontiac Grand Am and Buick Skylark are assembled in Lansing, Mich.

TOYOTA Camry LE Sedan

Japanese and American politicians should shut up and go away. Failing that, they should at least shut up on matters of trade — until they both decide to speak the truth.

Toyota Camry LE

Some Japanese politicians would have us believe that theirs is an open market.

Baloney.

The *total* foreign share of Japan's new-car market works out to a lousy three percent. That's barely a toe in the door, let alone a seat at the table.

Some American politicians would have us think that "buying American" will solve our economic problems.

More baloney.

Too many of Capitol Hill's pinstriped patriots preach red-white-and-blue consumerism, while sharpening regulations to cut the competitive standing of the very American industries they claim to support.

It's easy to get trapped in this madness and make choices based on the bias of the moment. It's easy, but wrong, particularly in a marketplace where intelligent consumer choices can be made solely on the quality and value of the products offered.

Take, for example, the Toyota Camry LE sedan. It's a darned good family car, which is not to say that it's perfect. It's a contender, which means that anyone shopping for a reliable, comfortable family sedan should look at it along with everything available in its size/price category.

Most U.S.-sold Camry cars are, after all, made in the United States. They are built by the same kinds of Americans who build Buicks, Chryslers and Fords. I know some of those people personally; and I don't know one

Complaints: Inadequate four-cylinder (standard) engine

Praise: A *must-shop* mid-sized sedan

Head-turning Quotient: Definitely attractive

Ride, Acceleration, Handling: Excellent

Brakes: Excellent

Suggested Retail Price: Around $20,000

Mileage: About 23 MPG

U.S. Content: 60%

of them who doesn't want to do a good job for their public, which is a heck of a lot more than I can say for politicians on either side of the Pacific.

Background: The current Camry cars, redesigned from top to bottom in 1992, constitute the third generation of a family car line that gets better with each revision.

The latest Camry models are taller by an inch, longer by six inches, and two inches wider than their predecessors. They are prettier, too — not an insignificant factor in a market where soul, as much as nuts-and-bolts quality, plays a major role in consumer decisions.

The Camry sedan has four trim levels — a base DX, mid-level LE, upscale XLE, and sporty SE.

Lower-level Camry cars come with a standard 2.2-liter, four-cylinder, 16-valve engine rated 130 horsepower at 5,400 rpm with a maximum torque of 145 foot-pounds at 4,400 rpm. Upper-level Camry cars get Toyota's 3-liter, 24-valve V-6 rated 185 horsepower at 5,200 rpm with a maximum torque of 195 foot-pounds at 4,400 rpm.

A five-speed manual transmission is standard in the base Camry DX (4-cyl.) and the base SE (V-6) sedans. A four-speed automatic is standard in all other Camry models.

All Camry sedans are front-wheel-drive, five-seat automobiles.

Complaints: The Camry sedan's standard four-cylinder engine is an adequate flatlands runner; but it's a wimp in the highlands at high speeds. Go for the V-6, which proved to be an all-around nice performer in tested 1993 and 1992 Camry LE sedans. Another gripe: In getting bigger, the Camry has grown fatter A, B, and C pillars — the posts that support the front, center and rear sections of the roof. That fatness sometimes obscures the driver's peripheral vision.

Praise: Excellent overall build quality and interior comfort; simple, excellently presented and easily readable instrument panel; height-adjustable front shoulder harnesses; standard driver's air bag; huge trunk; full-size spare tire. The Camry LE is a *must-shop* in the mid-size sedan category.

Head-turning quotient: Definitely attractive. Yet another bit of motorized proof that passion does not have to die with matrimony, mortgages, and middle-school PTA meetings.

Ride, acceleration, handling: Excellent ride and handling, especially on reasonably smooth roads and in tight curves. Both test cars were equipped with four-wheel, independent, McPherson strut suspensions. Still, both cars were bounced out of their comfort zones on rough streets and highways.

Acceleration: Take that 130-horsepower, four-cylinder engine and shove it! Give me the 185-horsepower V-6 instead, especially for traveling high-speed roads such as Detroit's portion of Interstate 75.

Braking was excellent. V-6 Camry sedans come with standard power four-wheel discs. Four-cylinder models get power front discs/rear drums. Anti-lock brakes are optional.

Mileage: As noted in the 1993 Camry LE V-6 sedan — about 23 miles per gallon (18.5-gallon tank, estimated 414-mile range on usable volume of 89-octane unleaded), running mostly highway and driver only.

Sound system: In the 1993 Camry LE V-6 — Six-speaker AM/FM stereo radio and cassette with graphic equalizer, Toyota Premium ETR. Bodacious boogie.

Price note: Toward the end of the 1993-model year, the Toyota LE V-6 sedan carried a suggested retail price of $20,078 with a dealer's invoice of $16,966. That price was moving — upward. Increasingly tough competition in the mid-size car segment, particularly from the Mitsubishi Galant and Nissan Altima and Chrysler's LH cars, will keep pressure on Toyota to moderate price boosts in 1994. That means it will be possible to get a decently equipped Camry for under $19,000 in the new year.

Coming changes: The Camry sedans get a two-door coupe stablemate in 1994. The engine of choice in that model will be the 3-liter V-6. The 1994 Camry sedan — all 1994 Toyota cars, in fact — will have dual-front air bags and ozone-friendly R-134A refrigerant.

Hometown: Most Toyota Camry models sold in the United States are built by Toyota Motor Manufacturing Inc. in Georgetown, Ky.

TOYOTA Camry LE Wagon

The vehicle was an ellipsoidal nightmare, a work of perfectly imperfect circles, a rolling ode to ovals. It was ugly.

It was the Toyota Camry LE wagon, introduced late in the 1992-model year.

No matter how I looked at it — from the front, sides, or rear — it came out odd, which was baffling. Here was a stylistic sibling of the beautiful, popular Toyota Camry sedan. How could it possibly look like this?

I was tempted to leave the wagon alone. But there was something about it....

I don't know.

Maybe it was a lifetime of parental warnings against judging by

Toyota Camry LE Wagon

You can still get a well-equipped Camry wagon for under $20,000 in 1994.

appearance. I drove the thing. I was surprised.

The Camry LE wagon turned out to be an exceptional vehicle, even with the four-cylinder engine I found so wimpy in the Camry LE sedan. It had something to do with expectations.

The LE sedan *looked* like a righteous runner. I figured it should run the way it looked — which it did in V-6 form. But with the four-cylinder engine, the LE sedan was as disappointing as a kiss-only honeymoon.

The four-cylinder wagon, though, was something else. It looked like a classic blind date — homely to the max, bereft of conversation and libido.

I didn't expect much. As a result, I was smiling when I got substantially more than I expected.

The test wagon's ugliness diminished with each mile behind its wheel. Affection displaced disgust. At the end of my scheduled time with the thing, I didn't want to give it back.

That was in August 1992. Since then, I've driven several Camry wagons, including a 1993 LE V-6. They were all as ugly as the first one. But I learned to look past that. I learned to love them.

Background: The first Camry wagon, introduced in the United States in 1986, was a linear affair. The new Camry wagons, the base DX and the more expensive LE, sacrifice aesthetic form for aerodynamic function, which is why they look like something from the Star Trek School of Design.

The DX runs with Toyota's 2.2-liter, four-cylinder engine rated 130 horsepower at 5,400 rpm, with a maximum torque of 145 foot-pounds at 4,400 rpm. The LE wagon gets the 3-liter, 24-valve V-6 rated 185 horsepower at 5,200 rpm with a maximum torque of 195 foot-pounds at 4,400 rpm.

Camry wagons, like the sedans, are front-wheel-drive, five-passenger vehicles. All Camry wagons come with four-speed automatic transmissions as standards equipment.

Complaint: I don't like the rear-facing third seat in the Camry LE wagon and in other wagons, foreign and domestic, not even with the outboard-mounted shoulder harnesses and seat belts included in the Toyota. Rear-facing seats often are less well-constructed than regular seats. Anyway, especially for children, they just don't seem the safest place to be in rear-end collisions.

Praise: Overall excellent vehicle build. Anti-noise engineering gets kudos. Hollow structural areas adjacent to the roof's edge are filled with foam rubber to help reduce wind noises. Also: A driver's air bag is standard, as are four-wheel disc brakes in the LE V-6 wagon. Power front discs/rear drums are standard in the four-cylinder DX and LE models. Antilock brakes are optional.

Cargo space is excellent — 40.5 cubic feet with rear-facing seat down and 140.8 cubic feet with both the rear-facing seats and the second-row seats folded.

Head-turning quotient: Future schlock. This is one case where traditional styling would've been better.

Ride, acceleration, handling: A surprising triumvirate of excellence, even with the four-cylinder package. However, if you routinely haul lots of people and lots of stuff, get the LE V-6.

Braking was excellent.

Mileage:
• In the 1993 four-cylinder DX — about 27 to the gallon (18.5-gallon tank, estimated 490-mile range on usable volume of regular unleaded), running mostly highway with three occupants and light cargo.
• In the 1993 LE V-6 — about 23 per gallon (18.5-gallon tank, estimated 415-mile range on usable volume of 89-octane unleaded), running mostly highway and driver only with 500 pounds of cargo.

Sound system: Eight-speaker AM/FM stereo radio and cassette with compact disc. Toyota Premium system. Excellent.

Price note: Toward the end of the 1993 model year, the LE V-6 wagon had a sticker price of $21,448 and a dealer's invoice of $18,124. The DX was running at $17,468 with a dealer's tab of $14,760. Upward price pressures exist here, too, especially inasmuch as the Camry is a popular wagon. But this is a highly competitive segment. You can bargain, and you can still get a well-equipped Camry wagon for under $20,000 in 1994.

Complaints: Rear-facing third seat

Praise: Anti-noise engineering. Excellent cargo space

Head-turning Quotient: Future schlock

Ride, Acceleration, Handling: All excellent — but a full load needs the V-6

Brakes: Excellent

Suggested Retail Price: $21,448

Mileage: About 23 MPG for the V-6 LE

U.S. Content: 60%

Coming changes: Toyota and other Japanese auto-makers have been changing models every four years. The Camry wagon was completely redone in 1992. Next big changes coming in 1995/1996. But the Camry wagon, like all Toyota cars, will have dual-front air bags and ozone-friendly R-134A refrigerant in 1994.

Hometown: The Camry wagons, like the sedans, are assembled in Georgetown, Ky.

3

Hot Dates Saturday Night

Affordable Sports Coupes & Convertibles — $13,000 to $23,000

CHEVROLET Cavalier RS Convertible

With Notes on the PONTIAC Sunbird SE Convertible

Summer threatened to end as strangely as it began — unseasonably cool weather, lots of rain. But the weather people were predicting a favorable change in the final days — sunshine, mild temperatures. It was convertible time.

I wanted something simple. Not simple like a Mazda Miata. You can drop the top on that one easily; but there's something precious, almost dainty about it.

I wanted a blue-jeans convertible. I chose the Chevrolet Cavalier RS.

It was funky metal — a red car with a tan interior and white top. It looked good to me; but I would've preferred a black or tan convertible roof. The white top/red body was reminiscent of buckskin shoes.

What the heck. There is something about a convertible that makes everything okay. It's the gentle flirtation with recklessness — the controlled rush of driving without the security of a hardtop. For me, it's more wind-in-your-face than wind-in-your-hair. My hair's wonderfully tight and curly — the wind couldn't move it, not even at hurricane force.

The Cavalier RS convertible was perfect for the moment. It was a just-folks, straightforward convertible that allowed me to take full advantage of

Praise: Power tops and four usable seats	
Head-turning Quotient: Nothing much	
Ride, Acceleration, Handling: All quite decent	
Brakes: Good	
Suggested Retail Price: Around $16,000	
Mileage: About 23 MPG with the 3.1L V-6	
U.S. Content: 90%	

Chevrolet Cavalier RS

the glorious respite from the summer's erratic climatic ways. A few, cool, sunlit hours — going nowhere in particular for no reason at all, with the wind rushing about. Truly, joy is where you find it.

Background: The first Chevrolet Cavalier convertible, introduced in May 1983, was something of a dog. It shared the woof pound with its sibling Cavalier coupes and sedans, which entered the market as 1982 models.

But all of the Cavaliers — and their like-bodied cousins, the Pontiac Sunbirds — have improved since those awful early days. They are solid, decent cars that, with a bit of tweaking, could be exciting.

The Cavalier RS and Sunbird LE convertibles prove that much. I drove the 1992, 1993 and 1994 versions of those cars. Only modest equipment and cosmetic changes separate those models.

The 1994 Cavalier, for example, gets an improved 2.2-liter, four-cylinder engine, redesigned rear brake drums, and some cosmetic changes in the front and rear fascias. The Sunbird gets similar treatment.

Both convertibles are tightly built, competent automobiles. They are fun. They made me smile; and if you're a convertible bargain hunter, they'll make you smile, too.

The standard engine in the 1994 Cavalier RS and Sunbird LE softops is a 2.2-liter, inline four-cylinder engine rated 120 horsepower at 5,200 rpm with a maximum torque of 140 foot-pounds at 3,200 rpm.

That is slightly better performance than found in the 1993 version of General Motors Corp.'s 2.2-liter inline four, rated 110 horsepower at 5,200 rpm with a maximum torque of 130 foot-pounds at 4,200 rpm. GM engineers claim that the extra power in the 1994 engine comes with a bonus — better fuel economy.

Both convertibles can get the optional 3.1-liter V-6, rated 140 horsepower at 4,200 rpm with a maximum torque of 185 foot-pounds at 3,200 rpm.

Get the bigger engine. Mate it with the standard five-speed manual transmission, General Motors Corp.'s Level II "Touring suspension," and four fat, 15-inch performance blackballs. That combination, in either the Cavalier or Sunbird, will give you one hot runner.

Complaints: Only applicable to the 1993 four-cylinder Cavalier RS and Sunbird LE convertibles, with their softer-than-thou Level 1 suspensions. These are wimpmobiles, the motorized equivalents of tie-dyed Tee-shirts.

Also, still no air bag after all these years.

Praise: The fun of it all and the ease with the power tops on both models go up and down. Praise also for four usable seats in both convertibles, for the installation of standard anti-lock brakes (with power front discs/rear drums), and for trunk space (10.7 cubic feet) that allows you to carry several bags of party goods.

Head-turning quotients:
- Cavalier RS convertible — attractive enough to invite friendly looks.
- Sunbird LE convertible — attractive enough to invite friendly looks and a little conversation

Ride, acceleration and handling: All quite decent in the V-6/Level II versions, thank you. All quite boring, even on the prettiest days, in the Inline Four/Level I (base suspension) models.

Braking, however, is good in all models.

Mileage: With the 2.2-liter, four-cylinder engine and five-speed manual transmission — about 25 to the gallon (15.2-gallon tank, estimated 370-mile range on usable volume of regular unleaded).

With the 3.1-liter V-6 and five-speed manual — about 23 to the gallon (15.2-gallon tank, estimated 340-mile range on usable volume of regular unleaded).

Sound system: As noted in the 1993 Cavalier RS convertible — optional Delco-Loc II system with AM/FM stereo and compact disc. Excellent.

Price note: GM has paid for the tooling on the Cavalier and Sunbird cars, which means the company is getting bucks on every one it sells. It also means that GM can keep the lid on 1994 prices on these cars, thus keeping the base stickers for both Cavalier RS and Sunbird SE convertibles

Attractive enough to invite friendly looks and a little conversation.

under $16,000.

The idea is to use these and other Cavalier/Sunbird cars to build volume sales, a tack which is working quite well for the Cavalier, but not as well for the Sunbird.

Coming changes: No major changes for 1994. These are carryover cars.

Hometowns: The Chevrolet Cavalier and Pontiac Sunbird convertibles are built in Lordstown, Ohio. Some Cavalier models are built at GM's plant in Ramos Arizpe, Mexico. But GM plans to move production of those models to Michigan by 1995.

Complaints: No air bags. Door-mounted safety belts

Praise: A truly affordable sports coupe

Head-turning Quotient: Lordy!

Ride, Acceleration, Handling: Whoa! It's fun! Excellent handling

Brakes: Very good

Suggested Retail Price: $18,675

Mileage: About 24 MPG

U.S. Content: 75%

CHEVROLET Lumina Z34

The Chevrolet Z34 was torch red with a louvered hood. I fell in love with it instantly.

It had big, 16-inch tires — Goodyear Eagle GT+4 radials — that hugged the road like you want to be hugged when only a hug will warm you. And it had chromed, dual exhaust pipes and brushed aluminum wheels, which shone brilliantly against its red body.

Lordy! It had some kind of an engine, too — strong, smooth, powerful.

Some engines just go vroom, vroom; they go fast, but leave you feeling disconnected to what's going on. The Z34's 3.4-liter, 24-valve, 210-horsepower V-6 went vroom, vroom, too. But It gave good torque, 215 foot-pounds at 4,000 rotations per minute. You felt it.

This was the kind of Chevrolet that Chevrolet's marketers must've been thinking about when they came up with their "Heartbeat of America" slogan, which ought to be changed to the "Heartbeat of North America" in the case of the Z34, inasmuch as the thing's built in Canada.

Anyway, the car got my heart pumping. It was totally funky — so funky, it brought back memories of the famed '57 Chevy Bel Air. It even had a back bench seat!

The Z34 had its shortcomings, of course; but I was willing to live with those. Love is like that, see? Ain't nothin' that sizzles that can't splatter grease; ain't nothin' that's hot that can't burn. Love ain't perfect, but in the case of the 1994 Chevy Z34, it's worth the risk.

Background: The Chevy Z34 is really a Chevrolet Lumina, but I have

Chevrolet Lumina Z34

emotional difficulty saying "Z34" and "Lumina" in the same breath. Regular Lumina models flirt with mediocrity. They are nice, reliable, front-wheel-drive family cars, decently styled; but there's little about them that's exciting or memorable.

The Lumina becomes interesting only in its Euro version, a good "Saturday night car"; and in its top-of-the-line Z34 dress.

The Z34 is sold only as a coupe.

The Euro is sold as a coupe and sedan — with the sedan being the more interesting of the two.

The Euro coupe is stuck with an engine shared by the more pedestrian Lumina models — a 3.1-liter V-6 rated 140 horsepower at 4,400 rpm with a maximum torque of 185 foot-pounds at 3,200 rpm. The Euro sedan gets, as an option, the powerful 3.4-liter, 24-valve V-6 sold as standard equipment in the Z34.

Complaints: No air bags. Door-mounted safety belts that grab your neck and, sometimes, catch you by the forehead. Also, the Z34's designers made a notable effort to make something of the narrow, strip-like, gauge package common to the Lumina line. But no sorcery can turn that particular sow's ear into a silk purse.

Praise: The Z34 is a blue-jeans special — a truly affordable sports coupe. It's a solid, well-constructed road-runner, quite comfortable for five occupants. I really enjoyed driving this one. What a hoot!

Head-turning quotient: The high and mighty thought it gaudy. The hip and cool shouted, "Lordy!"

Ride, acceleration and handling: Whoa! It was fun! Braking was good, too. Brakes include standard, power four-wheel-discs with anti-lock backup. Handling was excellent. I found myself hunting for curves in the Z34.

Mileage: About 24 to the gallon (16.5-gallon tank, estimated 386-mile range on usable volume of required premium unleaded), running mostly highway and driver only.

The Z34 comes with a standard, four-speed, electronically controlled automatic transmission.

Price note: 1994-model pricing was not firm at this writing. But it is unlikely to rise much above 1993 closing base sticker of $18,675, with a dealer's invoice of $16,341. The Z34 will be under pricing pressure from the new Chevrolet Camaro and Pontiac Firebird, both of which offer substantial performance, and more updated styling, at base prices below that of the Z34.

Coming changes: The 1994-model year most likely marks the last run for the Lumina Z34. Chevrolet is readying its replacement, the 1995 Monte Carlo coupe, scheduled for a fall 1994 introduction. Mechanically, the Monte Carlo will imitate the Z34, right down to the use of the double-overhead cam 3.4-liter V-6. Stylistically, the Monte Carlo will be rounded in the manner of a Ford Taurus.

Besides styling, important updates in the 1995 Monte Carlo will include dual-front air bags and, probably, the use of an environmentally friendly refrigerant in the air conditioner.

Current Chevrolet plans are for the Lumina to survive as a sedan; but the sedan also will receive a Taurus-like revision for 1995.

The 1995 Lumina sedan, to be introduced in early 1994, will include dual-front air bags and an updated version of General Motors Corp.'s widely used 3.8-liter V-6.

Hometown: The Chevrolet Lumina Z34 coupe is made in Oshawa, Ontario.

EAGLE Talon TSi

With Notes on the Mitsubishi Eclipse GSX

I left in the pre-dawn Georgia darkness, heading north towards Virginia. It was rainy, foggy—unseasonably cool. It made little sense to rise and run so early, especially on so wacked-out a morn.

But I had to get back to Virginia; and I figured that the All-Wheel-Drive Eagle Talon TSi sports coupe would get me through the mess okay and that, maybe, the weather would be better farther north.

Good guess.

Rain turned to brilliant sunlight at the North Carolina border; and the Talon TSi, which had moved through the muck with admirable dexterity, was running like crazy on the dry, clear roads.

I was happy—until horror sucked joy out of the trip. In the southbound lane of I-95, a Ford F-150 pickup truck had flipped on its roof. It was one of those ridiculously big-wheeled trucks, the kind with its body raised several feet above ground to accommodate gargantuan tires.

There were ambulances and police vehicles. A coroner's wagon was there, too, with its rear doors open, ready to receive somebody's shortened dream.

I found an exit after seeing that. I went to a Wendy's and ordered a hamburger, hot and juicy, and a chocolate frosty thing. I sat near a window and watched some young people ooohing and aahhing over the plum-red Talon TSi. I sat and watched and wondered about their dreams, and hoped that their hopes would never end on a highway on a beautiful day that began in the rain.

Background: The Eagle Talon, introduced in 1990, began life as an affordable sports coupe, a car for buyers who are "young, single, college-educated men and women seeking image-defining personal transportation" and who are looking for "performance on a budget," according to Chrysler's publicists.

Mitsubishi's publicists could've written the same thing inasmuch as their company designed the Eagle Talon TSi and sells the same car as the Mitsubishi Eclipse GSX.

The cars have changed little since their introduction; and they aren't changing much for 1994—which is too bad. Given their targeted buyers, the Talon and Eclipse should be entering the new model year with at least a driver's air bag. They're not.

Instead of bags, the cars come with front automatic seat belts and knee bolsters under the dashboard. That meets current federal safety standards. But the Talon and Eclipse are such otherwise excellent little cars, it's a pity that they don't exceed mandated safety goals.

Complaints:	No air bags. Useless rear seats
Praise:	A *hot* pocket-rocket
Ride, Acceleration, Handling:	Excellent, but bumpy
Brakes:	Excellent
Suggested Retail Price:	Around $15,000
Mileage:	About 23 MPG
U.S. Content:	73%

Eagle Talon TSi

Two of the hottest-

running, best-

styled pocket-

rockets on sale.

For 1994, product changes in the Talon/Eclipse cars include new gas-pressure shock absorbers with the all-wheel-drive models, and improved locks on rear seat belts to help retain child-safety seats.

The Talon is offered in three trim levels—base DL, more upscale ES, and the totally raucous TSi. The Eclipse is offered as a Base coupe, an upscale GS version, and the hot-dog GSX. The top-level TSi/GSX models are available as all-wheel-drive cars. The others are front-wheel-drive.

The base engine for both the Talon and Eclipse is a 1.8-liter, inline four-cylinder whippet rated 92 horsepower at 5,000 rpm. Maximum torque is 105 foot-pounds at 3,500 rpm.

A normally aspirated 2-liter, 16-valve, inline four-cylinder engine is standard for the Talon ES and Eclipse GS. That engine is rated 135 horsepower at 6,000 rpm with a maximum torque of 125 foot-pounds at 5,000 rpm.

The Talon TSi and GSX get a turbocharged version of the ES/GS engine rated 195 horsepower at 6,000 rpm with a maximum torque of 203 foot-pounds at 3,000 rpm.

A five-speed manual transmission is standard in all Talon/Eclipse models. A four-speed automatic is optional.

Theoretically, the Talon and Eclipse can seat four people; but that's just a theory. Only the two front seats are available for real people.

Complaints: No air bag and useless rear seats.

Praise: The Talon/Eclipse are two of the hottest-running, best-styled pocket rockets on sale.

Ride, acceleration and handling: Excellent acceleration and handling in the tested 1994 Talon TSi AWD. The ride is bumpy, despite the employment of an electronically controlled suspension system that can tune the ride to "soft" or "sport.'

The tested Talon TSi can become a crampmobile for anyone taller than five-feet, seven inches. But, hey, braking is excellent. Standard brakes include vented front discs/solid rear discs. Anti-lock brakes are optional.

Mileage: In the tested Talon TSi, about 23 to the gallon (estimated 350-mile range on usable volume of recommended premium unleaded), running mostly highway and driver only with light cargo.

Sound system: Optional six-speaker AM/FM stereo radio, cassette and compact disc with graphic equalizer, by Mitsubishi. Excellent.

Price: The Eagle Talon ended the 1993-model year with retail prices ranging from $11,752 to $17,772. Dealer invoice prices were from $10,957 to $16,435. Mitsubishi Eclipse prices ranged from $11,859 to $21,799. Dealer invoice prices were from $10,375 to $18,970, according to figures compiled by Auto Invoice Service in San Jose.

Why the higher Eclipse prices? A few more options. Not much else. Certainly nothing to justify that kind of price differential.

Prices will rise slightly on these models in 1994. But the Talon and Eclipse are *surrounded* by competition. You can bargain.

Hometown: The Eagle Talon and Mitsubishi Eclipse are assembled by Diamond-Star Motors, operated by Chrysler and Mitsubishi in Normal, Ill.

FORD Mustang

The horse is back.

It's on the grille of a Ford Mustang car, where it belongs.

More important, it's in the spirit of the new Mustang, running full gallop through the car's engineering and styling.

This is no small feat.

The horse disappeared from the Mustang's body in the early 1980s, but it vanished from the car's soul much earlier.

In place of the horse, Ford put its oval corporate logo, which was appropriate.

FORD
Mustang

Complaints: None, yet

Praise: It captures the the spirit of the original

Head-turning Quotient: Yessir! A standing ovation

Ride, Acceleration, Handling: Excellent

Brakes: Excellent

Suggested Retail Price: $11,000 - $21,000

Mileage: About 20 MPG

U.S. Content: 95%

Ford's logo, back then, stood for doing things by the numbers.

It stood for tumescent corporate ego and flaccid committee logic.

It damned sure didn't stand for quality, imagination, or guts.

By 1974, for example, the Mustang had become a wimpmobile, a truly underwhelming piece equipped with a standard 2.3-liter, inline four-cylinder, 88-horsepower engine. The car was an embarrassment to veteran Mustangers; but it was motorized opium for the masses, who bought 277,846 of those models, the Mustang II's.

Ironically, that "success" hurt the Mustang's image.

Too many Mustang II cars were trash — lousy fit and finish; lousy, unreliable standard engine; lousy handling. Mustang sales fell to 201,370 in 1975 and continued downhill until 1979, when Ford introduced an all-new model.

The 1979 Mustang platform remained in use through 1993, helped along by favorable sheet-metal changes and powertrain enhancements that brought back some of the car's former glory.

But there was no horse.

Until now.

The horse is back, and it's ready to run.

Background 1994: The 1994 Mustang is Madonna with manners, Mike Tyson with breeding — hot enough to get you going, but polite enough to ask if you want to go all the way. And if you wanna go that route, well, hooahh! There are two new Mustangs — the base and the luxury-sport GT — to get you there.

Both cars are front-engine, rear-drive models capable of seating four adults. Both are available as coupe or convertible.

Not available for 1994 is the Mustang's LX trim line — the old "base" car. Ford scrapped the three-door Mustang hatchback, too.

Getting rid of the hatchback and limiting the Mustang's body styles to coupe/convertible allowed engineers to build a stiffer underbody for the new car. That allowance, in turn, helped them to improve the new car's suspension for better ride and handling.

Standard in the base 1994 Mustang is a new 3.8-liter V-6 engine rated 145 horsepower at 4,000 rpm. Maximum torque is 215 foot-pounds at 2,500 rpm. The new V-6 replaces the workaday 2.3-liter, 105-horsepower, inline four-cylinder engine standard in the 1993 Mustang.

The new Mustang GT gets a 5-liter V-8 rated 215 horsepower at 4,200 rpm with a maximum torque of 285 foot-pounds at 3,400 rpm. That's 10-less horsepower and 15-less foot-pounds of torque than found in the 5-liter V-8 in the 1993 car. Big deal. The new Mustang GT is so tight, right, and aerodynamically correct, it can do 0-to-60 mph in a quite impressive 6.7 seconds.

A five-speed manual transmission is standard in the new Mustangs.

Ford Mustang

An electronically controlled four-speed automatic is optional.

Standard brakes are power, four-wheel discs. A four-wheel, anti-lock system is optional.

Dual, front air bags are standard in the new Mustangs.

Complaints: None, yet.

Praise: Ford's engineers and designers get top honors for developing a new Mustang that so wonderfully captures the spirit of the original 1964 car.

It doesn't matter that you might've never set foot in an early Mustang. Once you get behind the wheel of the new car, you will understand immediately what the original was all about — unabashed, All-American road-running at a reasonable price.

Head-turning quotient: Yessir! Look at this thing. Ford could've screwed up and come out with an all-things-generic, aerodynamically boring, butter-soft-lines, is-this-a-Japanese-car? remake of the Mustang. It could've slipped and gone front-wheel-drive; or gotten crazy and gone Rambo with all kinds of wanna-be-Lamborghini-but-don't-know-how junk.

Ford's Mustang team could've done all of those things had they not talked to the people who made the Mustang famous — the car's buyers.

For one thing, the buyers said they wanted the horse back — right, smack-dab center-grille, where God wants it.

Also, the buyers wanted an aerodynamically efficient body; but they didn't want function to overwhelm form, particularly that part of the form that is distinctly Mustang. So, the new car's cabin has a dual cockpit, just like the original model. The exterior body is rounded in keeping with 1990s functionalism; but it has all of the right Mustang touches, including the air scoops immediately behind the rear doors.

A standing ovation for styling.

Ride, acceleration, handling: The Mustang remains a car designed for mass consumption — a mandate that, in the past, was met by embracing the lowest common denominator and squeezing it until it collapsed in an orgasm of mediocrity.

No more.

Both the 1994 base and GT Mustangs offer excellent ride and handling. The base car will do nicely for those drivers who want to feel "sporty" without driving that way. The GT will please all but the most recalcitrant throttle jockeys, who probably shouldn't be allowed on public roads anyhow.

Of the models driven on Ford's test track in Dearborn, Mich., my favorite 1994 Mustang is the GT with its 5-liter V-8 with a five-speed manual transmission. Ride and handling in that model were exceptionally good. Brakes, including the optional anti-lock system, were excellent.

Mileage: In the 1994 Mustang GT, five-speed manual — about 20 miles per gallon (15.4-gallon tank, estimated 298-mile range on usable volume of regular unleaded), all test-track and driver-only, running at speeds and pushing the revs in a way that neither reflects sanity, nor real-world driving.

Sound system: The new Mustang will be the first car in the United States to be sold with a MiniDisc (MD) as a factory-authorized and dealer-installed option. This new system, the Mach 460, comes with three amplifiers driving eight speakers — four tweets, four woofs. You've gotta hear this thing. Bigtime boogie!

Price: The Ford Mustang closed the 1993-model year with prices ranging from $10,860 to $21,000, and with dealer invoice paper stamped at $9,796 to $18,821. Ford spent $700 million developing the 1994 Mustang. Most assuredly, the company will do its damnedest to recoup that cost.

But Ford intends to recover its investment and gain income through volume sales of the new Mustang. That means 1994 prices will be up, but not up enough to frighten prospective buyers away — which means that you oughtta be able to pick up a new Mustang and still have something left for Saturday night.

Hometown: The first 1994 Ford Mustang is scheduled to roll of the assembly line in Dearborn, Mich., on Monday, Oct. 4.

FORD Probe

With Notes on the Mazda MX-6

The designers called it "Rio red," which meant nothing to me, except that it was pretty. Even the jaded garage people, who've driven and seen everything, admitted as much.

It went like that all week. People liked the new Ford Probe, a front-engine, front-wheel-drive sports coupe designed by Ford and engineered and built by Mazda. And the people who owned older Probes, wow!

There was this young woman who pulled up next to me in a black 1990 Probe LX. My peripheral vision caught her stare, which I was determined to ignore. But she yelled through her open window into my open window and, well, I couldn't ignore that.

"That's the new Probe?" she asked.

"Yep," I said tersely.

"You like it?" she asked.

"Yep."

"Looks good," she said. "You have a chance to do anything with it, yet?"

I assumed she meant speed, which meant I couldn't give her an honest answer.

"Nice car," I said, seeking refuge in evasion.

"Yep," she said, and left when the light turned green.

Background: Ford introduced its first marketable Probe as a 1989 model. The qualifier is needed because the original Probes actually were concept cars displayed at auto shows. The Probe name, controversially unorthodox in automotive nomenclature, described the mission of those experimental vehicles — built to "probe" the future.

The Probe is based on the same platform as the Mazda MX-6 sports coupe. Both cars, extensively reworked for the 1993-model year, also share the same engines.

There are two Ford Probes for 1994, a base model and the perfor-

Complaints: Bouncy. Rear seats too small

Praise: Overall excellence. Common-sense instruments

Head-turning Quotient: Nothing much

Ride, Acceleration, Handling: Decent

Brakes: Excellent

Suggested Retail Price: Around $20,000

Mileage: About 24 MPG on V-6 models with 5-speed standard

U.S. Content: 77%

Built to "probe"

the future.

mance GT. The base car is equipped with a 2-liter, four-cylinder, 16-valve engine rated 118 horsepower at 5,500 rpm with a maximum torque of 127 foot-pounds at 4,500 rpm. The GT comes with a 2.5-liter, 24-valve V-6 rated 164 horsepower at 5,600 rpm with a maximum torque of 160 foot-pounds at 4,800 rpm.

The base Mazda MX-6 gets the 2-liter, four-cylinder job; the MX-6 LS coupe gets the 2.5-liter V-6.

Despite plenty of similarities, the Probe and MX-6 have their differences. The Probe is, ahm, stiffer. Seriously. Ford's engineers dialed in a bit more "road feel" in the Probe, attempting to give it bona fide sporting manners. Mazda's people went the other way, taking a softer and somewhat more enjoyable approach to life.

Complaints: The Probe's engineers increased the structural rigidity of the new car and revised the front suspension to get a lower, swoopier front end. That helped to create a stunning machine that runs beautifully on smooth roads. But all of that tightening bounces butts on less-than-perfect thoroughfares.

On the other hand, while offering a generally smoother ride, the MX-6's handling sometimes swerves towards boredom. What can I say? You can't please anybody.

Also, theoretically, the Probe and MX-6 are designed to seat four people. But only your theories will fit in the rear seats.

Praise: Both the Probe and the MX-6 are excellent overall sports coupes. Instrument panels in both cars are designed with common sense, making them easier to use and see. Dual-side air bags are standard in both cars for 1994, as is the use of environmentally friendly air-conditioner refrigerant (free of ozone-destroying chloroflourocarbons).

Anti-lock brakes are optional.

Power four-wheel-disc brakes are standard on the uplevel Probe and MX-6. Power front discs/rear drums are standard on the base models.

Head-turning quotients:
• Probe — fine.
• MX-6 — damned fine.

Ride, acceleration and handling: Excellent smooth-surface ride in the Probe. Rough-surface ride in that car is bothersome. Very good all-around ride in the MX-6. Excellent all-around handling in the Probe. Very good to wimpy handling in the MX-6.

Both the four-cylinder and V-6 engines deliver excellent acceleration; but the V-6 leave you smiling longer.

Braking is good in both cars.

Mileage: Take a breath. Okay? Here goes:
• In the four-cylinder models equipped with standard five-speed manual transmissions — about 30 to the gallon (15.5-gallon tank, estimated

Ford Probe

455-mile range on usable volume of regular unleaded);

• In the four-cylinder models equipped with optional four-speed automatic transmissions — about 27 miles per gallon (15.5-gallon tank, estimated 409-mile range on usable volume of regular unleaded);

• In the V-6 models with standard five speed — about 24 to the gallon (15.5-gallon tank, estimated 362-mile range on usable volume of recommended premium unleaded);

• In the V-6 models equipped with optional four-speed automatic transmissions — about 23 to the gallon (15.5-gallon tank, estimated 347-mile range on usable volume of recommended premium unleaded).

Sound system: As noted in the tested 1994 Ford Probe GT — optional AM/FM stereo with compact disc and graphic equalizer, Ford Premium Sound. Good boogie.

Price note: Again, prices on Japanese-nameplate cars have been rising faster than prices on domestic nameplates, and probably will continue to do so in the 1994-model year. Mazda MX-6 prices tend to be higher than those on comparable Ford Probes, and that also is likely to remain the case in 1994. Still, buyers of Ford Probes and Mazda MX-6 models should be able to get those cars, reasonably well-equipped, at prices below $20,000 in 1994.

Advice: Cool it on the options. They can really rock your wallet.

Insurance note: Even with driver air bags, insurers tend to charge high rates for Probe and MX-6 sports coupes. Why? Young buyers. Crash-loss and theft-loss experience. Insurers do it by the numbers.

Hometown: The Probe and MX-6 are assembled in Flat Rock, Mich. by AutoAlliance International Inc., a joint-venture company operated by Ford and Mazda.

Complaints: Rear seat too small

Praise: Overall excellent construction

Head-turning Quotient: Passionate Puritanism

Ride, Acceleration, Handling: All excellent

Brakes: Excellent

Suggested Retail Price: $16,000 - $23,000

Mileage: About 23 MPG

U.S. Content: 96%

FORD Thunderbird

With Notes on the Mercury Cougar XR7

Life with Ford Thunderbirds has been like life with long-term house guests — swell beginnings, lots of excitement.

The excitement wears off. Shortcomings are exposed — chief among them, lack of space.

In the house, the space shortage leads to bungled bath schedules. No one wants to use the cramped and inadequate downstairs powder room, the wood and dry-wall equivalent of the T'Bird's rear cabin. Everyone wants to use the upstairs bathroom at the same time.

Tempers flare, as they do in the Thunderbirds.

But the flareups in the T'Birds are worse. Five people are packed into a space that is best suitable for two normal-size people up front and two tiny types in back. There's no way for anybody to get away from anybody. People stew, with most of the steam rising from the cars' rear quarter.

This situation won't change with the modestly redesigned 1994 Thunderbird.

The new car has the same interior dimensions as the 1989 Thunderbird, the platform on which the 1994 model is based. To wit: front head room is 38.1 inches and front shoulder room is 59 inches. Ditto the 1993 model. Rear-occupant space, with a minimum 35.8 inches of leg room, also matches up in the new and old cars.

But Ford has rearranged the interior of the 1994 model, redecorated it if you will. The wraparound instrument panel is new and fresh. It seems to embrace the driver. The front-passenger compartment has been converted into a pleasant oval, replete with a standard passenger air bag. It all seems quite homey up there. But the rear cabin remains the same.

Still, the car's redesign gave me an idea of how to ease life with future

Ford Thunderbird

house guests.

We can redecorate upstairs, make it feel more open and roomy. And we can do to the downstairs powder room what Ford should've done to the new T'Bird's rear cabin — make it bigger and more usable.

Failing those things, we simply can tell prospective guests the truth: "You're welcome for short stays. But only two of you will fit."

Background: The Ford Thunderbird was first introduced in the fall of 1954 as a 1955 model. It since has gone through several changes and, in the process, has kept company with the good, the bad, and the ugly in automotive design.

The current generation Thunderbird was introduced in 1989. Though short of interior space, the 1989 model was long on passion. It was a good looker and runner, and both of those virtues have been passed on to the 1994 car.

The Thunderbird comes two ways, as the luxury LX and the supercharged SC sports coupe. The LX is equipped with a standard 3.8-liter, sequentially fuel-injected engine rated 140 horsepower at 3,800 rpm. Maximum torque is 215 foot-pounds at 2,400 rpm.

Fuel-injection systems electronically monitor the amount of fuel delivered to the combustion chamber. The idea is to increase engine power while limiting fuel consumption through precise metering. Multi-point and sequential fuel injectors do this job best.

The T'Bird is a

"Saturday Night

Special" of a

different sort. A

personal

luxury/performance

car, strictly driver

oriented.

A four-speed automatic transmission is standard on the 1994 LX.

The supercharged SC comes with a standard, supercharged, sequentially fuel-injected, 3.8-liter V-6 rated 210 horsepower at 4,000 rpm with a maximum torque of 315 foot-pounds at 2,600 rpm.

Superchargers are engine-driven devices that push more air and fuel into the combustion chamber to produce more power. As a result, a supercharged V-6 can deliver as much, or more power than a normally aspirated — regular breathing — V-8. But keep in mind that superchargers increase engine complexity and maintenance costs, and that they also can reduce fuel economy.

To help control fuel consumption, a five-speed manual transmission is standard on the SC. A four-speed automatic is also available.

For 1994, Ford's modular 4.6-liter, sequentially fuel-injected engine is available as T'Bird optional equipment. The engine is rated 190 horsepower at 4,200 rpm with a maximum torque of 260 foot-pounds at 3,200 rpm.

The Thunderbird is a front-engine, rear-wheel-drive coupe.

Complaints: Interior rear-passenger space. Enough said.

Praise: The T'Bird is a "Saturday-night special" of a different sort. It is a personal luxury/performance car, strictly driver-oriented, with some allowable enjoyment for the front-seat occupant. Overall construction is excellent. The dual-front air bags and other 1994 functional changes, including environmentally friendly air-conditioner refrigerant, make sense.

Traction control and anti-lock brakes are optional.

Head-turning quotient: A work of passionate Puritanism — a swoopy, aggressive front-end that says, "Come here"; a reserved rear-end that says, "Stay away."

Ride, acceleration, handling: Ride for two front occupants is excellent; awful for anyone else. Acceleration with any of the three T'Bird engines available is excellent. Braking was excellent in the tested 1994 LX.

The test car was equipped with optional power four-wheel discs with anti-lock backup. (Those brakes are standard on the SC.) Standard LX brakes are power front discs/rear drums.

Mileage: In the tested 1994 LX with the standard 3.8-liter V-6 — About 23 to the gallon (18-gallon tank, estimated 404-mile range on usable volume of regular unleaded), running mostly highway and driver only.

Sound system: In the tested 1994 LX — AM/FM stereo radio and cassette, Ford Premium system. Very good.

Price note: The Thunderbirds flew out of the 1993-model year at prices ranging from $16,000 to $23,000. They will fly into the 1994 model year at a slightly higher price, largely because of new equipment.

Companion car: There is no practical difference between the Ford Thunderbird and the Mercury Cougar XR7. Both cars are built on the same platform; both share the same engines and drive-trains, with the exception of the supercharged 3.8 V-6 exclusive to the T'Bird SC.

Like the Thunderbird, the Cougar XR7 has new front and rear exterior cosmetic work for 1994. The interior front cabin also has been redone, partly to accommodate new standard, dual-front air bags. Other new standard items include an electronically controlled, four-speed automatic transmission and Chloroflourocarbon (CFC)-free air conditioner refrigerant.

Hometown: The Thunderbird and Cougar are assembled in Lorain, Ohio.

PONTIAC Firebird Formula V-8 & Chevrolet Camaro Z28

They are the essence of tumescence, cars designed in a high-school boy's locker room. They're so self-consciously virile, they call attention to themselves wherever they go. They are rock videos on wheels, provocative to the max, bound to raise eyebrows among the self-anointed saints of social consciousness, certain to excite the libidos of adolescents aged 15 to 50.

Introducing the 1994 Pontiac Firebird Formula V-8 and the 1994 Chevrolet Camaro Z28, cars so out of sync with the politically correct 1990s, so blatantly rebellious in execution, they are destined to attract buyers.

I mean, let's get something straight: few things about the new Firebird and Camaro embrace responsibility. This is as it should be. This is why I love them.

Firebirds and Camaros — General Motors Corp.'s famous F cars — were never responsible. They were celebrations of perennial youth — rolling icons to audacity. Their sales declined dramatically in the last decade, not because that spirit died, but because GM strayed and got iconography mixed up with the making of junk.

The young and the restless — prime buyers of hot metal — resent rattles. But too many of the old F cars rattled to hell and back.

No longer.

If the tested Firebird Formula V-8 and Camaro Z28 are representative,

Complaints: Small trunk, micro rear seats, limited front-seat head room

Praise: Two of the best, most-exciting sport coupes under $20,000

Head-turning Quotient: Your place or mine?

Ride, Acceleration, Handling: Good to excellent

Brakes: Excellent

Suggested Retail Price: Formula V-8: $17,995
Z28: $16,779

Mileage: About 19 MPG

U.S. Content: 73%

GM stayed with

what it knew —

and improved the

hell out of it.

GM's new F-series is as tight and right as it is wild and sexy. You can strut your stuff in these cars without worrying about your parts falling off.

Background: The very first F cars hit the market in the fall of 1966 to do battle against the Ford Mustang. The Firebird and Camaro did okay in that fight, racking up a combined total of nearly 300,000 sales in 1967 alone. In 1979, production of those cars exceeded the 400,000 mark. F-car sales remained strong into the early 1980s; but their numbers fell below 80,000 sales in 1992, raising ominous speculation about their future.

Age, federal fuel-economy and safety regulations, along with stale design and sloppy construction, caught up with the F cars.

They had become fat caricatures of their former selves — like two beer-bellied, 60-year-old men running around in leisure suits and gold chains. They seemed welcome only in those places where beer bellies were acceptable, giving them a kind of underclass patina that didn't show well to the general public.

Making the F cars' decline all the more visible was the emergence of smart, new sports coupes, such as the Ford Probe GT, Nissan 240SX-SE, Toyota Celica GT, Honda Prelude Si, and Dodge Stealth.

While studying ways to meet that competition, GM flirted with some radical F-series changes, including proposals to convert the traditionally rear-wheel-drive Firebird and Camaro to front-wheel-drive.

Going to front-drive would've taken some weight out of those cars. But a cash-short GM nixed that idea as too expensive — and too risky. The relatively few people who were still buying Firebirds and Camaros loved the rear-drive layout — viewed it, in fact, as the only way to get a scream out of anything called a "performance car."

Going to front-drive would've blown those folks away, with no guarantee that a front-wheel-drive F car would've been strong enough to attract new buyers. So, GM stayed with what it knew — and improved the hell out of it.

Though still rear-drive, the new Firebirds and Camaros are extensively redone — 90-percent new parts in all. Besides the rear-drive arrangement, only the rear axle and a part of the rear floorpan are carryovers from previous models.

The new cars are longer, wider, and taller than their predecessors. Their roofs, doors, hatches and spoiler assemblies are made of a tough, lightweight sheet molded compound (SMC). Use of that material gives the new F-car bodies cleaner, more uniform designs.

Composite materials also are used in the front fenders and the front and rear fascias. The cars have been made tighter with the use of high-tech adhesives and better-conceived construction techniques, such as the welding of the rear quarter panels to the frame of the cars.

The Firebird comes in three iterations: Firebird (base), Formula, and

Pontiac Firebird Formula V8

Trans Am. The Formula and Trans Am are equipped with the Corvette-derived, 5.7-liter, LT1 V-8 engines, rated 275-horsepower at 5,000 rpm with a maximum torque of 325 foot-pounds at 2,400 rpm. The base Firebird comes with a 3.4-liter V-6 rated 160 horsepower at 4,600 rpm with a maximum torque of 200 foot-pounds at 3,600 rpm.

The Formula and Trans Am have standard *six-speed* manual transmissions. The base Firebird runs with a standard five-speed manual. A four-speed automatic is optional in the base Firebird.

Chevrolet Camaros come two ways — base and Z28. The base car is equipped with the standard 3.4-liter V-6 and five-speed manual. The Z28 has the 5.7-liter V-8 and six-speed manual. A four-speed automatic is available for the base Camaro.

Demographically, the upscale Firebirds and Camaros are aimed mostly at single males with annual incomes over $40,000. The base cars target mostly college-educated women with incomes over $35,00. Go figure.

Other than styling — pop-up headlamps for the Firebird, fixed quad lamps for the Camaro — there is very little difference between the two cars.

Complaints: The Firebird/Camaro trunk is practically non-existent — deep and wide enough only for a few garment bags. Ditto the F cars' two rear seats, which are useful only for very short and skinny people.

Both cars have 68-degree slanted windshields, which are great for exterior looks. But some tall people, and at least one short one, complained that the design robbed them of head-space.

Praise: Easily two of the best, most exciting sports coupes available at base prices below $20,000.

Standard equipment is impressive, and some of it is even adult. To wit: dual front air bags, anti-lock brakes, computerized "Pass-Key" anti-theft system, Solar Ray glass, 16-inch aluminum wheels — and environmentally friendly refrigerant in the air conditioning system.

Head-turning quotients:
• Pontiac Firebird Formula V-8 — Your place, or my place?
• Chevrolet Camaro Z28 — My place.

Ride, acceleration, handling: Ride is good in both cars. Handling is excellent. Acceleration? Both the Formula V-8 and Z28 kick lots of tailpipe — maybe, too much. At 65 miles per hour in fifth gear, the engines in both cars are barely turning 2,000 rpms. In sixth, you can zip past 80 mph with little notice. Not good. You want to be aware of doing something that stupid.

Front and rear power disc brakes are standard on the Formula V-8 and Z28. Trust me. They're good brakes. Anti-lock power front discs and rear drums are standard in the base cars.

Sound system: In the tested Formula V-8 — ten-speaker, AM/FM stereo radio and cassette with 5-band graphic equalizer, Delco/Bose music system. In the tested Z28 — AM/FM stereo radio and compact disc with digital seek-scan, Delco-Loc II system. Both will blow your mind.

Mileage: Thirsty beasts. About 19 per gallon (15.5-gallon tanks, estimated 280-mile range on usable volume of recommended super unleaded), running mostly highway and driver only.

Price note: Toward the end of the 1993-model year, the Formula V-8 had a base price of $17,995 and a dealer invoice of $16,465. The Z28 was running at a base of $16,779 with a dealer invoice of $15,353. These are high-demand cars. Expect some 1994 price increases up to $200 per car.

It remains to be seen whether insurers will buy GM's argument that the new Firebird and Camaro deserve at least an "average" insurance rating. Some insurers say they will give discounts for the dual-front air bags and other safety devices found in the new F cars. But, ultimately, rates will be set based on insurer's claims experience with those models. Here's hoping that the standard anti-theft devices work, and that new Firebird and Camaro owners practice safe driving.

Coming changes: New Camaro and Firebird convertibles, available in base and uplevel models, for 1994.

Hometown: The Firebird and Camaro are assembled in St. Therese, Quebec. That's not exactly "from the country that gave you rock and roll." But, hey, it's close enough.

4

Livin' Large

Complaints: Too many power adjustments for driver's seat. Sideview mirrors too small
Praise: A superior long-distance runner
Head-turning Quotient: It gets you respect
Ride, Acceleration, Handling: Excellent ride and acceleration. Handling leaves something to be desired
Brakes: Good, but give yourself some space
Suggested Retail Price: $29,395
Mileage: About 23 MPG
U.S. Content: 90%

BUICK Park Avenue Ultra

With a note on the Oldsmobile Ninety-Eight

It was a serious car, midnight blue with gray interior. It had a fine body, Jaguaresque in appearance. But the dark paint muted the sensuality of that shape. Even the bright molding, wrapped around the car's lower panels, seemed bereft of levity.

Still, I liked the thing, the new Buick Park Avenue Ultra. I liked sitting in it. It had big, comfortable, leather-faced seats. And it was neat the way the instrument panel curved around the front end of the passenger cabin until it disappeared into the doors.

But I felt a little strange in the Park Avenue Ultra on the Saturday I drove it. Saturday is get-funky time. But it's hard to get funky in a car that prefers pin stripes over denim. So I wore a blazer and dress shirt with my jeans, and cranked up the engine.

You should've heard that engine! It was deep and throaty — kind of made me smile. I mean, here was this car, all proper and everything, with an engine that sounded like a love scene between Madonna and Arnold Schwarzenegger. Hoooah!

I headed for I-95, bound for New York. The car could move. I was having a good time until I pulled into the parking lot of a public rest stop.

Buick Park Avenue Ultra

Church people were getting off a bus that identified them as church people. Some of them stopped to admire the Park Avenue Ultra, which looked clerical in repose.

"Beautiful car, young man," one of the church ladies said. I glowed. Forty-five years old and chubby, and some woman's calling me "young man." I sucked in my gut, for naught. "You a minister?" she asked.

Background: Buick did a major revision of the Park Avenue in 1991, changing the car to front-wheel-drive and jettisoning its boxy lines in favor of soft curves and elegant roundwork.

In 1992, Buick brought forth the Park Avenue Ultra with a new, supercharged, 205-horsepower version of General Motors Corp.'s 3.8-liter V-6 engine.

In 1994, the Ultra gets another boost — a reworked, supercharged 3.8-liter V-6 rated 225 horsepower at 5,000 rpm with a maximum torque of 275 foot-pounds at 3,200 rpm.

Talk about throaty! The new engine growls and groans so much, it ought to come with a parental advisory.

The 1994 Park Avenue and Park Avenue Ultra also get standard dual-front airbags, the installation of which required some redesign of the dashboard. But the flowing, wraparound lines of the interior that made the 1991 Park a hit are still there.

The Park Avenue is the top-of-the-line Buick; the Ultra is the top-of-

Insurance companies offer rate discounts on the Park Avenue models.

the line Park Avenue.

Complaints: My perennial whine about the new-generation Park Avenue concerns the driver's seat (way too many power adjustments) and the sideview mirrors (too small, oddly shaped, and oddly angled). Those beefs hold true for the 1994 model.

Praise: Excellent overall design (I really love this car); a superior long-distance runner. Kudos to Buick for making the second air bag standard. High-fives for the other standard stuff, including anti-lock brakes and automatic climate control. Traction control, to limit wheel slippage, is available.

And, hey, listen up: insurance companies offer rate *discounts* on the Park Avenue models, partly because of the cars' safety engineering, but also because the people who buy them tend to be mature sorts who obey traffic rules.

Head-turning quotient: The Ultra gets you respect even when you don't want it.

Ride, acceleration and handling: Excellent ride and acceleration.

Handling — even with the tested Park Avenue Ultra's FE3 "special handling" suspension — might leave something to be desired among people accustomed to the taut responsiveness of German luxury cars.

Brakes — power front discs/rear drums with anti-lock backup — are very good. The Ultra is *big* It stops smartly, but not as smartly as you might want it to stop in close-drill, wet-weather braking. Give yourself some space.

Mileage: About 23 to the gallon with the improved Ultra V-6, remarkably close the the mileage of the 205 horsepower V-6 engine. Tank capacity is 18 gallons. Estimated 403-mile range on usable volume of recommended premium unleaded, running mostly highway and driver only.

Sound system: AM/FM stereo radio and compact disc player, Delco/Bose Music System, easily among the best automotive sound systems available.

Price note: The Park Avenue Ultra sedan closed the 1993 model year with a sticker of $29,395 and a dealer's invoice of $25,427. The base Park Avenue was priced at $26,040 with a dealer invoice of $22,525. Additional 1994 equipment will boost those prices. But Buick lately has been an aggressive marketer, giving discounts when needed to move metal.

Companion car: The Oldsmobile Ninety Eight Regency is the nuts-and-bolts soulmate of the Buick Park Avenue. The differences primarily are stylistic. The Park Avenue is prettier by yards. In 1994, the Ninety-Eight gets dual air bags, too. The Ninety-Eight Touring Sedan, the Park Avenue Ultra-equivalent, also gets the upgraded, supercharged 3.8 V-6.

Hometowns: The Buick Park Avenue is made in Wentzville, Mo. The Oldsmobile Ninety Eight is assembled in Lake Orion, Mich.

CADILLAC Coupe DeVille

*Say goodbye. It's going home
To that place
Where old cars roam.
It's been around since '49,
Sometimes ugly, sometimes fine.
In '93, 'twas front-wheel-drive,
But still too long, still too jive
For Baby Boomers
Who thought a coupe
Should have less length,
And lotsa swoop.
So, to DeVille, we bid "Adieu"
And hail replacement spanking new
The Cadillac Concours
A four-door deal,
Big of heart, big of wheel.
The Concours gets Northstar V-8
With horsepower not quite as great
As horses in the Eldo Coupe.*

Cadillac Coupe DeVille

That was planned. It ain't no bloop.
The '94 Concours, Caddy's car
Linking small to biggest star — the Fleetwood,
A thing of such whopping gait,
It, too, gets a new V-8.
The Concours resembles the STS,
Smaller, sporty, a Caddy best.
The Concours, too, is front-wheel drive
With lots of stuff to keep alive
The driver and those who ride,
Folks at risk when cars collide.
Dual air bags? Yes. And anti-lock brakes,
And traction control to escape mistakes,
And leather seats, fine stereo,
Cupholders and space for five to go.
More Concours news?
We gotta wait.
The car's still rolling
Toward the gate.

Complaints:
Road noise

Praise: An excellent commuter

Head-turning Quotient:
Cute. No rush

**Ride, acceleration,
handling:** Decent

Brakes: Excellent

Suggested Retail Price:
$11,195

Mileage: Very good — about
32 MPG

CADILLAC Eldorado Touring Coupe

It was the night of the vampire moon — big, round, silver-bright, seductive, yet forbidding. 'Twas a nocturnal beauty that bade me park the car along a back road skirting the Chesapeake Bay. But there was more fear than communion in that space. I kept the motor running.

Though, in retrospect, the motor hummed as much out of companionship than preparation for flight. It was the 32-valve Northstar V-8, the new engine in a number of Cadillac cars, including the Eldorado Touring Coupe in my possession.

The car served as talisman; the humm-thrumm of its engine became a rap mantra, a monody sung to ward off evil spirits:

Cadillac Eldorado Touring Coupe
Beaucoup curves, lotsa swoop
Low-slung hood that's plenty hip
Sassy fine tail that's just as flip

Bright chrome moldings gone monotone
Lord! Looky here — a telephone!
Ain't no vamp gonna take this ride
Let the walkin' dead walk
While the living folks glide

Crazy? Yeah. But it was a kind of craziness born of childhood in black New Orleans, with all of its talk of voodoo rituals in Old Congo Square. Even the most Catholic among us had respect for those superstitions, frowned upon by the Church but deeply imbedded in our culture and folklore.

It was all coming back that night at the bay, with its moonlit waves glistening in the distance, its chilled air and hints of ultimate loneliness. It felt good, at that instant, to be connected to something as finite and controllable as the Eldorado Touring Coupe. And it felt good, too, to turn back onto the road and to head toward the main highway with all of its cars and trucks — and its people behind the wheels.

Background: I've always loved Cadillacs, even when they were the big ol' funky things of the 1970s and 1980s, hung with chrome-covered gimcrackery and every other sort of nonsense. I particularly loved the Eldorado, with its blatantly gangster looks, highlighted by a rear "sail pan-

Cadillac Eldorado

el" that Cadillac, thankfully, has retained in the newer models.

However, in the 1970s and 1980s, my love for the Cadillac marque often was reactionary — sort of like the defense of a friend or a relative who is no longer wonderful to be around. Hell, I knew that things had hit rock-bottom for Cadillac in the early 1980s when the night-life vamps and their masters of illicit trade began trading in their "Eldo's" and Coupe DeVilles (discontinued for 1994) for BMW and Mercedes-Benz Cars.

How things have changed!

Step inside the Eldorado Touring Coupe with its well-crafted interior of leather and Zebrano wood; its instrument-panel design that rivals anything from Lexus, Audi, BMW or Mercedes-Benz; and its absolutely splendid 4.6-liter, 32-valve Northstar V-8, rated 295 horsepower (versus 270 horsepower for the ne Concours) at 6,000 rpm. Maximum torque is 290 foot-pounds at 4,400 rpm. This is Cadillac resurrected!

The Eldorado Touring Coupe remains pretty much the same in 1994 as it was in 1993, when it received the Northstar V-8; and as it was in 1992, when it was radically redesigned. The new model has a relocated seat lumbar control, moved from the center console to the driver's seat itself; and a softer suspension for 1994.

The Eldorado Touring coupe is a two-door, front-wheel-drive, four-passenger car.

Complaints: The design of the Eldorado Touring Coupe's super-aero body is a bit too clever. It greatly reduces wind resistance; but by having windows that practically disappear into the roofline, it also increases the chances of wetting front-seat occupants if there's any water on the roof when the windows are lowered.

Also, the rear "sail panel" I love so much is artful. But in terms of rear vision, it's sometimes obtrusive.

Praise: The Eldorado Touring Coupe easily ranks among the best luxury road cars — a standing enhanced by its relatively "low" luxury price. This car has practically everything — dual air bags for front occupants, an electronically controlled suspension system, and automatically heated front windshield to ease the task of winter de-icing, power four-wheel disc brakes with anti-lock backup, overall high-quality construction and a sumptuous passenger cabin designed within the bounds of good taste.

Head-turning quotient: A body so beautiful, it raises the sap in humans awake and vamps at nap. Beware of the attention that this one brings. Be wary of vamps — and uniformed things.

Ride, acceleration and handling: Cadillac's engineers once figured that the Eldorado's buyers would be hip enough to appreciate a hard, BMW-type ride. The buyers were hip, but their butts were soft, and they didn't appreciate the hard ride one bit. To placate those people, Cadillac softened the Touring Coupe's ride for 1994. There also have been some

Its interior rivals anything from Lexus, Audi, BMW or Mercedes-Benz. This is Cadillac resurrected!

adjustments in steering feel to please those motorists for whom the joy of driving has nothing to do with speeding down the Autobahn. Frankly, I can live with all of the adjustments in the 1994 car. Age has a way of changing one's definition of "thrill."

Braking is excellent in the Touring Coupe.

Mileage: Hee, hee, hee. Come, let me suck your fuel! About 23 miles per gallon (20-gallon tank, estimated 450-mile range on usable volume of required premium unleaded), running mostly highway and driver only with light cargo.

Sound system: AM/FM stereo radio and cassette with compact disc. GM/Delco Gold Series. Easy use. Great vibes.

Price note: Toward the end of the 1993-model year, the Eldorado Touring Coupe was priced at $39,590 (including the $5,000 Touring Coupe package), with a dealer's invoice of $34,084 (including $4,250 in dealer's cost for the Touring Coupe), according to Automobile Invoice Service. The regular Cadillac Eldorado, as the above price note indicates, was $5,000 less. GM is likely to keep the lid on its Touring Coupe prices in 1994 to help improve the somewhat sluggish sales of those models.

Hometown: The Cadillac Eldorado Touring Coupe is built at General Motors Corp.'s Detroit-Hamtramck plant in Michigan.

CADILLAC Fleetwood

Complaints: It's *big!*
Praise: Excellent craftsmanship
Ride, Acceleration, Handling: Soft and powerful, but take it easy on those curves
Brakes: Excellent
Suggested Retail Price: $33,990
Mileage: About 25 MPG
U.S. Content: 90%

I could never figure out the connection between ecclesiastical achievement and Cadillacs, such as the humongous Cadillac Fleetwood. But so many truly successful ministers owned big Cadillacs in my home state of Louisiana, I always assumed there must've been a divine linkage.

The "truly successful" ministers were those who pastored at brick and mortar churches purposefully built to be churches. Less successful reverends preached in storefront houses of worship.

The storefront preachers, even if they were doing well at the collection plate, usually drove Chevrolets or, at most, Buicks.

It was politics.

Big Cadillacs sent the wrong message to impoverished congregations, thus creating the kind of misunderstanding that could lead to vile and ruinous gossip about the pastor and his intentions.

But elite men of the cloth never worried about that sort of thing. In fact, their more prosperous flocks wanted them to drive Cadillacs, the bigger the better, as long as the car was painted a dignified black.

In retrospect, I guess it was a pride thing: big, long Cadillac parked in front of a pretty brick church; folks lingering around the car with the minister, chatting after services. Hmmmm. It sort of showed everybody that the congregation was blessed.

Background: It boggles the mind that General Motors thought it necessary to make the gargantuan Cadillac Fleetwood even bigger, but that is what the auto maker did when it redesigned the car for 1993. The new Fleetwood is 4.1 inches longer than its predecessor, meaning that the current model stretches 225.1 inches — 18.75 feet!

That makes the Fleetwood the longest regular production car built in America.

And for 1994, it will become the *most powerful,* longest regular production car built in this country.

The 1994 Fleetwood gets the Corvette-derived, 5.7-liter, LT1 V-8 rated 260 horsepower at 5,000 rpm with a maximum torque of 330 foot-pounds at 3,200 rpm. That's an extra 75 horsepower over the 5.7-liter V-8 in the 1993 Fleetwood. But that extra power comes with a bonus — improved fuel-efficiency because of the engine management systems used in the LT1 V-8.

Other changes in the 1994 Fleetwood include a revised, electronically controlled four-speed automatic transmission to handle the power of the new V-8, a recalibrated speed-sensitive steering system designed to eliminate some of the loose feel in previous Fleetwood steering systems, and some minor cosmetic alterations.

The Fleetwood is a rear-wheel-drive, six-passenger car with a big ol' trunk — 20.8 cubic feet.

Complaints: Look, I can accept the notion that cleanliness is next to godliness. But, hey, bigness? Does anybody anywhere need a car as big as the Fleetwood on a regular basis? I mean, anybody other than owners of limousine services and funeral homes, and ministers who believe that a tangible demonstration of success in the here and now says something about the probability of making it in the hereafter? Goodness, gracious, great wheels o' fire!

Praise: Bigness aside, the Fleetwood is an excellently crafted car. There was nary a rattle or jingle in the 1993 and 1994 models I drove. That's a heck of an achievement, considering the Fleetwood's body-on-frame construction and what that means for potential ill fits. Cadillac's use of one-piece stamped doors eliminated some rattle noise. Overall quality assembly did the rest.

Dual-front air bags and anti-lock, power front disc/rear drum brakes are standard in the Fleetwood.

Head-turning quotient: Your head turns for an eternity watching this one go buy.

Ride, acceleration, handling: The ride's so soft and comfortable, it makes you start humming hymns, like, "Swing, low, sweet chariot, coming for to carry me home."

Acceleration was excellent in the 1993 Fleetwood, and it's even better in the 1994 model.

But there's only so much that can be done with a giant car's suspension. The Fleetwood floats around curves with noticeable body roll. With this one, I bid ye to go gentle into corners, lest ye meet your maker sooner than planned.

Braking is excellent.

Mileage: In the 1994 Fleetwood with the LT1 V-8, about 25 to the gallon (23-gallon tank, estimated 560-mile range on usable volume of regular unleaded gasoline), running mostly highway and driver only.

Sound system: Six-speaker AM/FM stereo radio and compact disc with graphic equalizer. GM/Delco Bose. Excellent, as usual.

Price: Toward the end of the 1993 model year, the Fleetwood was priced at $33,990, with a dealer's invoice of $29,401. That price is likely to bump up a bit in 1994 with the addition of the new LT1 V-8 and the improved transmission. But, you can bargain on Fleetwoods.

Hometown: The Cadillac Fleetwood is made in Arlington, Texas.

Cadillac Fleetwood

CADILLAC Seville

Complaints: Clumsy turn-signal stalk

Praise: Nice design. Good seats

Head-turning Quotient: That's a Cadillac?

Ride, Acceleration, Handling: All excellent

Brakes: Excellent

Suggested Retail Price: $43,000

Mileage: About 23 MPG

U.S. Content: 90%

The 1992 model year started the fourth edition of Cadillac's Sevilles, which were introduced in 1976 as boxy bits of nouveau riche pretension. The new Sevilles — the base Seville and the sporty STS are far superior to their predecessors. Both product quality and design have improved substantially, making the Seville unapologetically competitive with the likes of the Lexus LS 400, the Infinity Q-45 and the Mercedes-Benz 300 series. Someone with taste has finally taken over Cadillac design.

Complaints: Cadillac needs to get rid of that all-in-one, multi-switch, wiper / turn-signal stalk in the STS. It's a clumsy gizmo that just doesn't fit. It would be nice if Cadillac could give us thinner A-pillars around the windshield. The car's overall sleek appearance is marred by those fat stanchions.

Praise: Excellent exterior / interior design. Kudos to the STS seats, front and rear. Deep, comfortable, yet exceptionally supportive seats. The front-wheel-drive, five-passenger car comes with dual air bags, anti-lock brakes and large, four-wheel, power disc brakes as standard equipment.

Head-turning quotient: Often-heard comments: "Pretty car" and "fancy car" and "that's a Cadillac?"

Ride, handling and acceleration: Comparable to and in some cas-

Cadillac Seville

es better than Lexus, Infiniti, Mercedes-Benz. The STS's automatic transmission is better than those found in the Mercedes 300 series and Mitsubishi Diamante.

The base Seville is equipped with a 4.9 liter, multi-point fuel-injected V-8 rated at 200 horsepower. No apologies here, either. The STS comes with the Northstar 4.6 liter, 32-valve, 295 horsepower V-8.

Sound system: AM / FM stereo radio, cassette and disc player — four speakers, 200 watts, boss-time boogie from Delco / Bose.

Mileage: About 23 to the gallon (18.8 gallon tank, estimated 432-mile range).

Price: Base price about $43,000, STS base $47,000.

Purse-strings note: Traditional Cadillac buyers will wince at the price, but this is no traditional Cadillac.

CHEVROLET Caprice

With a note on the Buick Roadmaster

He says he drives it "every now and then." He says he's careful, and we'd all like to believe my father when he says that. But he's in his "early eighties," and we worry.

He drives a 1978 Chevrolet Caprice, a big, brown, battle-scarred thing that he says "works fine."

We asked him to ditch the car in 1991, when General Motors gave the Caprice its first major redesign in 14 years. But my father, a recalcitrant left-brained sort, said, "No."

We asked again in 1993, when GM reworked the rear end of its new-generation Caprice — at long last giving it the rounded rear wheel-wells that consumers wanted on the 1991 car.

My father liked the new design; but, still, he wouldn't budge.

Maybe, he'll go for the '94.

The changes in the latest Caprice are incremental. They include two new engines for 1994, dual-front air bags, environmentally friendly R-134a air conditioner refrigerant, a standard PASS-Key II Theft-Deterrent System, and a beefed-up suspension to take some of the legendary squishiness out of the Caprice's handling.

Other than those things, the 1994 Caprice essentially is the same as the body-on-frame, rear-wheel-drive Caprice that Chevrolet "downsized" in 1977. My father's 1978 car is based on that model, a fact he's sure to

Complaints: Where 'ahm gonna park it, man?

Praise: Big enough for six large people. And that trunk!

Ride, Acceleration, Handling: A motorized manatee

Brakes: Excellent

Suggested Retail Price: Around $18,000

Mileage: About 24 MPG

U.S. Content: 90%

mention in resisting entreaties to buy a new one.

Dad's a strange dude. He's a retired science teacher whose done some extensive research in cellular biology, and he's always asking people — even at his advanced age — to present mountains of evidence before he decides anything.

My hunch is that the only way we'll get him out of his 1978 Caprice is that the car will go — or he will go to that great motorway in the sky.

Should Dad go first, I can imagine his interview at the Pearly Gates.

Gatekeeper: "You are Daniel Thomas Brown, Sr.?"

Dad: "Yes sir."

Gatekeeper: "For years, Mr. Brown, your loving family begged you to buy a new, improved Chevrolet Caprice. Much to their consternation, you refused. Why?"

Dad: "Hell, man. The old one worked."

Background: The full-size Chevrolet — variously named the Bel Air, Impala and Caprice — has been on sale since 1946. Every teacher and preacher in my family owned one, mostly because, as blacks in the segregated South, they needed a car big enough to serve as a motel and dependable enough to get them from Point A to Point B with no unplanned stops.

Times have changed and so has the full-size Chevrolet; though, as I've said, the basics of the car have remained the same. The 1994 model would look good in the driveway of my parents' suburban New Orleans home. And, Lord knows, the presence of standard dual air bags in the new car would help us all rest easier on those "every now and then" occasions when my father sneaks out of the house.

Engine details: A new 4.3-liter, sequentially fuel-injected V-8 replaces the 5-liter V-8 workhorse in standard Caprice models. The new engine is rated 200 horsepower at 5,200 rpm with a maximum torque of 245 foot-pounds at 2,400 rpm. The old 5-liter V-8 was rated 170 horsepower at 4,000 rpm with a maximum torque of 255 foot-pounds 2,400 rpm.

The new standard engine will go into the Caprice Classic and LS sedans and wagons.

But, to attract Caprice buyers younger than my father's generation, Chevrolet is offering something else for 1994 — the Corvette-derived, 5.7-liter V-8 rated 260-horsepower at 5,000 rpm with a maximum torque of 330 foot-pounds at 3,200 rpm.

The bigger engine will go into the — ha! — drum roll, pleeeeze — 1994 Impala SS sedan!

That's right — the Impala SS, the Impala, a name first used on a full-size 1956 Chevrolet show car that eventually went into production in 1958.

Chevrolet is banking on baby-boomer nostalgia (memories of summer

Chevrolet Caprice

nights in the back seat of a 1962 Impala SS 409 Sport Coupe) with its rein-troduction of the Impala SS. Besides the big engine, this special Caprice comes with a black-on-black paint treatment, a new grille, a rear-deck spoiler, Impala SS emblems, and a "Boyz in the Hood" attitude. Nahh, it ain't my father's Chevrolet.

Complaints: The Caprice sedans are so damned big, they're sinful. The cars ride on a 115.9-inch wheelbase — the centerline distance between the front and rear wheels — the longest wheelbase in the full-size car market.

Even with their redesigned backsides, I still have problems figuring out where the rear end stops when I'm backing up in a Caprice. Garage attendants hate these cars, as evidenced by the groans and mutters that greet me whenever I show up in one.

"Where 'ahm gonna park it, man? Where 'ahm gonna park it?" one Washington garage attendant asked when I pulled up in a 1994 Caprice Classic.

"Hell if I know," I said. I gave him the keys and walked away.

Praise: The size. The Caprice is a big, strong car that can seat six big, strong people comfortably. (The Impala SS is designed to carry five very large people comfortably.)

And, whoa! That trunk. At 20.4 cubic feet, it's big enough to carry the contents of a small house.

Nahh, it ain't

my father's

Chevrolet.

Hats off to Chevrolet for getting dual air bags and anti-lock brakes into the 1994 Caprice models as standard equipment.

All Caprice models, sedans and wagons, have standard, electronically controlled four-speed automatic transmissions.

Head-turning quotient: Your head would've turned a full 360 degrees by the time a full-length Caprice passed by.

Ride, acceleration, handling: The 1994 Caprice Classic's larger rear shocks (35 mm versus 25 mm in the 1993 model) eliminate some of the car's squishiness — but not enough to encourage foolish behavior around curves. It still wiggles a bit in deep turns.

The tested 1993 Caprice Classic, with the standard 4.3-liter V-8, zoomed along nicely down the highway, a motorized manatee moving at speed.

Braking — power vented front discs/rear drums with anti-lock backup — was excellent.

Mileage: About 24 to the gallon (23-gallon tank, estimated 540-mile range on usable volume of regular unleaded), running mostly highway and driver only.

Sound system: Optional AM/FM stereo radio and compact disc with coaxial speakers, GM/Delco. Big-boom boogie, heavy on the base. Very good.

Price note: Toward the end of the 1993-model year, the Caprice Classic sedan had a sticker price of $17,995 and a dealer invoice of $15,746. The relatively modest changes in the 1994 model probably will put the sticker firmly in the $18,000 range. But considering what's being offered, that's okay. Higher prices, of course, will attend to the Caprice LS and Impala SS. But those cars most likely will roll in in the lower $20,000 range, still a good price for the package.

Companion car: The Chevrolet Caprice and Buick Roadmaster are structural and mechanical twins. There's not a bit of substantial difference between the two cars, other than this: for 1994, only the Caprice gets the new 4.3-liter V-8. The Roadmaster gets the updated, Corvette-derived LT1 5.7-liter V-8 as standard equipment.

The 1994 Roadmaster also gets dual air bags and standard anti-lock brakes.

Hometowns: The Chevrolet Caprice and Buick Roadmaster sedans are built in Arlington, Texas. The Caprice and Roadmaster Wagons, and some Caprice sedans, are assembled in Willow Run, Mich. But GM, at this writing, is planning to move all Caprice/Roadmaster production to Arlington, Texas.

CHRYSLER New Yorker

With Notes on the Chrysler LHS

Complaints: Not yet	
Praise: A damned fine car	
Head-turning Quotient: Super sexy	
Ride, Acceleration, Handling: First-class	
Brakes: Excellent	
Suggested Retail Price: $24,294	
Mileage: About 24 MPG	
U.S. Content: 90%	

She came screaming into our room. Bob, my fellow boarder, jumped up. I bolted upright, too. She sat on the edge of his bed. She wore night skimpies. Bare-chested Bob wore shorts. She was crying. He was holding her.

"Give us a moment," Bob said.

"Yeah sure," I mumbled, and went downstairs.

This happened in the summer of 1969 at the Penington Friends House, a Quaker-run residence in New York City. Memories of that episode returned at the end of a recent visit to the city. I had come to cover the New York Auto Show, and was driving back in one of the displays, a 1994 Chrysler New Yorker.

It was a splendid machine, a beautifully shaped car with a high, oval roof. It was so New York — smooth, hip. The car reminded me of Bob. What a dude! He loved to talk. We loved to listen. He was our leader, the guru to us barely-20 types.

But Bob never told me what happened that night. I fell asleep on the parlor couch. The woman wasn't a regular boarder. I never learned her name; and I lost track of Bob when I moved out of the Penington.

Crazy, the way the mind works. I found myself looking out of the windows of the New Yorker on my way out of town, looking for that woman, looking for Bob. I didn't see them, of course. I probably would not have recognized them, anyway. Things change in two decades. The car I was driving proved that much.

Background: In 1990 I wrote a column on the "funereal Imperial," a vinyl-roofed, chrome-laden, squared-bodied, time-worn knockoff of the then-equally miserable Chrysler New Yorker. Lee Iacocca, Chrysler's chairman at the time, was so angered, he phoned me. He told me to high-tail it to Chrysler headquarters in Highland Park, Mich. I went. Lee chewed me out. I listened, I told him to build a better car. The dude turned crimson and shipped me over to Chrysler's design studio with an equally red-faced Chrysler public relations man.

But there in the studio was the wonder of wonders: a fleet of Chrysler prototypes, mock-ups of what today are Chrysler's Jeep Grand Cherokee and such passenger cars as the Chrysler Concorde, Dodge Intrepid, Eagle Vision and the brilliantly redone New Yorker.

The cars were unlike anything I had ever seen in a foreign or domestic studio. They were big without being cumbersome, luxurious without gim-crackery. There was nary a square line on them; and there was nowhere, absolutely nowhere where anyone could conceivably paste on a patch of vinyl roofing.

All of the cars were front-wheel-drive. The LH models — the Concorde, Intrepid and Vision — were designed as midsize automobiles. The New Yorker and the Sportier New Yorker LHS were based on the same platform as the midsize cars, but stretched to full-size dimensions with all of the appropriate adjustments in powertrain and suspension work.

"We had to push Lee to build these cars," a Chrysler design official said back then. "He wanted more squares. We told him, 'No.' It took some doing, but he finally gave us the go-ahead,"

Good for Lee. Good for Chrysler.

Complaints: At this writing, I really can't find anything that I dislike about the new New Yorker. I've racked up mileage on the auto show sample and several other 1994 New Yorkers. I'm sure there's a glitch there somewhere, something that will turn up in time.

Praise: The New Yorker comes standard with dual air bags and power four-wheel-disc, anti-lock brakes.

Overall design is excellent. For example, the front floor-pan of the car is angled upward to help keep front-seat occupants upright in frontal crashes. Traction control, to help prevent wheel-spin when accelerating on slippery surfaces, is optional. An electronically controlled, four-speed automatic transmission is standard.

The instrument panel is aesthetically pleasing, practically beautiful. All buttons and gauges are exactly where they should be.

Also, the 1994 New Yorker seats six adults without compromise. It has a humongous trunk — 17.9 cubic feet. And though the car is large, it is as tight as a nicely done sports coupe. It's a damned fine car, period.

Head-turning quotient: Super-sexy roofline. Snapped heads all over the place.

Ride, acceleration and handling: No wobble, no wallow. A first-class road-runner. The New Yorker is equipped with a standard 3.5-liter, 24-valve, V-6 rated 215 horsepower at 5,800 rpm. Maximum torque is 221 foot-pounds at 2,800 rpm — as much oomph as a lot of V-8 models.

Braking is excellent, as is road-holing in messy weather. But some of the credit here goes to 15-inch Michelin XW4 tires.

Mileage: About 24 miles to the gallon (18-gallon tank, estimated 421-mile range on usable volume of recommended 89-octane unleaded), running mostly highway, mostly driver-only with light cargo.

Sound system: Optional eleven-speaker, AM/FM stereo radio and compact disc. Chrysler/Infinity Spatial Imaging Sound System. Oh, yes!

Price note: Toward the end of the 1993-model year, the 1994 New Yorker carried a base price of $24,294, with a dealer invoice of $21,309, according to Automobile Invoice Service in San Jose, Calif. But Chrysler was planning to boost prices on those models by about $200.

Chrysler New Yorker

The New Yorker potentially can become a high-demand car. But that potential lies in its quality, content — and pricing. Several MBAs at Chrysler already have figured this out. Here's betting they're smart enough not to get greedy.

Companion car: The Chrysler LHS is the Chrysler New Yorker extremum. The LHS shares the same engine and drivetrains, but goes gaga with the extras. Those include items such as standard power moonroof, leather seating surfaces. top-line stereo system, fog lights, mini-overhead console, traction control, spiralcast wheels and power windows. Yet, Chrysler was smart enough to introduce the LHS at $29,046, nearly $1,000 under the $30,000-price limit before the federal government starts adding luxury taxes. Chrysler will bust its fiscal tail to keep the LHS under $30,000 in 1994.

Complaints: Boring

Praise: Exceptionally well-built

Head-turning Quotient: Not much

Ride, Acceleration, Handling: A "cush" car

Brakes: Excellent

Suggested Retail Price: $33,850

Mileage: About 24 MPG

U.S. Content: 97%

LINCOLN Continental

I dyed the gray out of my hair; but it didn't matter. I got the tint job the same week I got the 1994 Lincoln Continental Executive Series sedan, a car that symbolizes all things gray.

The Continental Executive is so formal, it creaks.

Not squeaks.

The car's built well. But it creaks. It's a spiritual thing.

For example, take the test car's interior: It's black with simulated walnut-wood inlays. "Map pockets," vinyl pouches, adorn the lower interior front-door panels. These pouches look like formal curtains hung upside down. The cabin feels like a boardroom after an executive coup.

Though sporting a new grille and taillamps, the Continental Executive's exterior isn't much better. It's formal to the max. Long and linear with meek curves at the rear. Drive it, or salute it? That is the question.

The Continental Executive is a luxury automobile, but it's luxury without poetry, life without passion. It's a business trip to Southern France without even a thought of blowing a day in St. Tropez.

Aarrgghh!

The next time I'm feeling hip enough to dye my hair, I'm going to make sure that a car like the Continental Executive isn't on the test schedule. I was ready to roll out and party. This car made me feel like I was about to take my final run.

Background: Lincoln Continental cars have been on sale in America since 1939. They *are* premium luxury cars, despite their excruciatingly stiff demeanor.

That's probably why Lincoln Continentals are so popular in U.S. government motor pools. They are swanky; but they don't convey the wrong impression. You've got to figure whoever's riding in one is going to work.

The Continentals were substantially redone for the 1988-model year. Current models — front-wheel-drive, four-door, six-passenger sedans — are based on the 1988 Continental platform.

There are two Continental models — the Executive Series and the Signature Series. The Signature Series — the very name indicates "personal" — is a friendlier, more likable car. Signature color schemes are more attractive and some of the interior appointments, notably the standard JBL Sound System, bespeak a willingness to please the individual.

Besides styling updates, other Continental changes for 1994 include a beefed-up suspension (rebound springs for front and rear suspension, eliminates some big-car squishiness), a new decklid closing mechanism, new electronically controlled seats in the Signature Series, solar glass to

Lincoln Continental

reduce cabin penetration of infrared rays, and environmentally friendly (CFC free) air conditioner refrigerant.

Both Continentals are equipped with Ford's 3.8-liter, sequentially fuel-injected V-6 rated 160 horsepower at 4,400 rpm. Maximum torque is 225 foot-pounds at 3,000 rpm.

Dual-front air bags and anti-lock brakes have long been standard items in the Continentals.

Complaints: A boring car that also needs a bigger engine.

Praise: An exceptionally well-built boring car that needs a bigger engine. The Continental Executive is comfortable for five people; but it's a little less comfortable for six.

Trunk space, 19.1 cubic feet, is good.

Oh, yeah, the insurance companies love this car, of course. Check the executive parking garage of almost any large insurance company, and you're sure to find at least three Lincoln Continentals there. The Continental gets a rate discount.

Head-turning quotient: With a chauffeur up front and smoked limousine windows, and official flags flying atop the front fenders, the Continental Executive attracts attention. Without those things, people assume that there's just another damned lawyer behind the wheel, and they look away.

Ride, acceleration, handling: Okay, okay, okay. Look, this is a clas-

An exceptionally well-built boring car.

sic American "cush" car. It's built to isolate its occupants from whatever is happening outside — which also accounts for its popularity in government circles.

Brakes — power four-wheel discs with anti-lock backup — are excellent.

Mileage: About 24 to the gallon (18.4-gallon tank, estimated 413-mile range on usable volume of recommended 89-octane unleaded), running mostly highway with one to six occupants.

Sound system: Electronic AM/FM stereo radio and cassette, Ford Premium Sound. What's a nice boogie box like you doing in a car like this?

Price note: In mid-summer 1993, the 1994-model Continental Executive was priced at $33,850 with a dealer's invoice of $28,695, according to Automobile Invoice Service in San Jose, Calif. The Continental Signature was priced at $35,750 with a dealer's invoice of $30,291. Calendar 1994 prices probably will remain at that level. Besides, you can bargain for sales discounts on these cars.

Hometown: The Lincoln Continental is assembled in Wixom, Mich.

Complaints: Restricted rear seating

Praise: Simply beautiful, inside and out

Head-turning Quotient: Whammo! Modern soul

Ride, Acceleration, Handling: All superior

Brakes: Excellent

Suggested Retail Price: $36,890

Mileage: About 23 MPG

U.S. Content: 95%

LINCOLN Mark VIII

There was work to be done. Writing. But the day was oh-my-God beautiful. There was a new Lincoln Mark VIII in the driveway. Write or drive? I chose to drive.

Varrrooommm, varrrooommm! I drove from Washington, D.C. to Baltimore; cranked the car up again and drove to Manassas, Va. Also drove to West Virginia, out near Harpers Ferry, where the roads are curvy and the police are, well, reasonable.

A West Virginia officer stopped me. Nice man.

"That a 'merican car," he asked.

"Yessir, sho is."

"Shoot! That's a pretty car," he said.

"Yessir, sho is. The new Lincoln Mark VIII."

"I see you're from Michigan," the policeman said, referring to the car's tags.

Silence. I smiled. I live in Virginia.

"You be careful out here," the policeman said, without ever requesting my license or reaching for a ticket.

Lincoln Mark VIII

"Yessir, sho will."

Really nice car. Really nice cop. Really close call. I figured it was time to get back to my laptop.

Background: The current Mark was introduced in December 1992 as a 1993 model. It came loaded with standard equipment, such as dual air bags and anti-lock, four-wheel-disc brakes, and Ford's modular 4.6-liter V-8. That left little for the company to do with the 1994 Mark VIII.

Changes, such as they are, include the addition of electronically controlled "memory" outside mirrors, and new Nudo soft-leather seats.

Since the birth of the Mark series in 1956 with the introduction of the Mark II coupe, the Mark often has served as Ford's rolling test bed, featuring items such as the first American-made overdrive transmission, the first standard electronic instrument cluster and message center, and the first keyless entry system.

The new Mark — outfitted with Ford's newest and, perhaps, best V-8 engine — continues that practice. The modular 4.6-liter V-8 is rated 280 horsepower at 5,500 rpm. Maximum torque is 285 foot-pounds at 4,500 rpm.

An electronically controlled, four-speed, automatic overdrive transmission is standard in the Mark VIII.

Complaints: The Mark VIII and Ford Thunderbird, though discernably different in numerous ways, are structural and mechanical cousins.

That means they both have restricted rear-cabin space. It also means they have a mutual disrespect for the proper placement of the parking brake pedal.

In both cars, the pedal juts out at an unfortunate angle on the driver's side, intruding into the cabin and presenting something of an obstacle to the left ankle.

Praise: A simply beautiful automobile, inside and out. The cabin literally envelopes the Mark VIII's four occupants, enclosing the front two occupants in maximum comfort.

The rear-seat people in the Mark VIII are not as cramped as their counterparts in the Thunderbird and Cougar, largely because the Mark is more purposefully designed to seat four people (instead of the ludicrous attempt to squeeze five normal-size people into the Cougar and T'Bird).

The Mark VIII's attempt to make life pleasant for the backseaters is commendable inasmuch as, like the Thunderbird and Cougar, it is a front-engine, rear-drive coupe — the kind of car that habitually treats front-seat occupants nicely while giving short shrift to the people in the back.

One of my favorite features in the feature-laden Mark VIII is the Auto-glide mechanism in the front seats, which automatically moves the front seats ahead when their seatbacks have been tipped forward. This allows back passengers to get in and out of the car without tripping all over themselves.

Also, at 14.4 cubic feet, Mark VIII trunk capacity is decent.

Head-turning quotient: Super-smooth front end accented by a hint of the famous Lincoln grille and slivers of wraparound headlamps. Then there's the rear end with its sexy, wheel-hump trunk lid. Whammo! Outta here! We're talking modern soul.

Ride, acceleration and handling: Some buff-book writers bow-wowed about how the Mark VIII gets a little dicey on race tracks at speeds exceeding 90 miles per hour. Who gives a hoot? For the way most of us drive, the Mark VIII's ride, acceleration, handling and braking are all superior.

The car's 4.6-liter V-8 has lots of low-end torque, which means that you can get a pretty good thrill without going over the hill on speed.

Mileage: About 23 to the gallon (18-gallon tank, estimated 400-mile range on usable volume of recommended premium unleaded), running mostly highway with one to four occupants and light cargo.

Price note: Toward the end of the 1993-model year, the Mark VIII had a sticker price of $36,890 and a dealer invoice of $31,273. Retail prices probably will hover around the $37,000 mark in 1994. But, fear not. A number of Lincoln dealers have shown some willingness to bargain on this one.

Hometown: The Mark VIII is assembled in Wixom, Mich.

MERCURY Grand Marquis LS

With a note on the Ford Crown Victoria

The Mercury Grand Marquis LS is an old folks' home, but that's okay. Lots of us have old folks we love. Besides, if we're lucky, those of us who are young and middle-aged today will be old folks soon enough.

That said, it's comforting to know that some auto makers have not totally abandoned the needs of the aging body in pursuit of young bucks. It's also nice to see some auto designers out there fighting the notion that old is the same as dead.

Time was when American big-car luxury meant square and boxy metal, accented with vinyl roofs and lots of chrome and brushed aluminum. You'd see these things going down the road, and you'd have to do a double take to make sure that the car wasn't part of a funeral procession.

That time is gone, if the 1994 Grand Marquis and its mechanical twin, the Ford Crown Victoria, are any indication. Both cars, extensively reworked in 1992, have pleasantly rounded bodies and more than a little hint of personality and rambunctiousness. But make no mistake about it, both cars are very conservative.

Step inside the 1994 Grand Marquis. A six-way power driver's seat nods to modernity; but it's part of a traditional split-bench arrangement. Other traditional notes include the velour "luxury cloth" covering the seats

Complaints: Boring instruments

Praise: Solid. Perfect for cross-country driving

Head-turning Quotient: Ho-hummer supreme

Ride, Acceleration, Handling: Triple aces

Suggested Retail Price: $22,690

Mileage: About 20 MPG

U.S. Content: 73%

Mercury Grand Marquis LS

and what Ford calls "woodtone appliques" applied to the instrument and door panels.

It's an old car in new metal. I didn't mind running around in it for a week. Running? Make that "strolling."

Background: Politics has a way of ruining tradition. Take the Grand Marquis. Once the quintessential "All-American" car, it now contains enough foreign parts to escape the technical definition of "domestic". The reason is the arcane politics of something called corporate average fuel economy (CAFE), the federal requirement that an auto maker's new-car fleet average 28.5 miles per gallon.

Big cars tend to bring down that average. Little cars tend to boost it.

The kicker is that an American car company cannot include its foreign-sourced little cars to raise its average.

Likewise, the government cannot use the company's foreign-sourced big cars to lower the company's CAFE standing and put it in jeopardy of paying stiff penalties.

Like many things political, it makes absolutely no sense.

The upshot is that Ford Motor Co. is using enough parts from Mexico, Germany and several other countries to make the Grand Marquis LS "foreign." Nifty, eh?

The Grand Marquis is a front-engine, rear-drive, six-passenger car. It comes two ways — the less-decorated GS and the more-decorated LS. The base engine is a 4.6-liter, sequentially fuel-injected V-8 rated 190 horsepower at 4,600 rpm, maximum torque is 260 foot-pounds at 2,600 rpm.

A 210-horsepower version of that engine is available, and is recommended for buyers who plan to tow trailers with the Grand Marquis.

Both the GS and LS have standard four-speed, automatic overdrive transmissions.

Complaints: Though reworked in 1992 and 1993, the instrument panel in the Grand Marquis remains boring. It's not quite an ergonomic disaster, but it seems totally disconnected from the modern theme of the car's exterior.

Praise: An overall solid big car, perfect for cross-country driving. Dual air bags were made standard in 1993. Dual, hydraulic power, four-wheel disc brakes are also standard. Anti-lock brakes with traction control are optional.

Head-turning quotient: Ho-hummer supreme.

Ride, acceleration, handling: Triple aces for the intended audience — people in their mid-fifties and early sixties, folks who are old enough to know that you don't have to drive like a darned fool to get where you're going if you leave on time. Hot rodders won't like it. But then, those perennially recalcitrant teenagers don't like much of anything that suggests life sometimes means growing up.

Mileage: In the tested Grand Marquis with the optional towing package, about 20 to the gallon (20-gallon tank, estimated 385-mile range on usable volume of regular unleaded), combined city-highway, running with one to five occupants and light cargo.

Sound system: Four-speaker AM/FM stereo radio and cassette, by Ford. Johnny Mathis and Nat King Cole never sounded better.

Price note: Towards the end of the 1993-model year, the Grand Marquis LS was sticker-priced at $22,690, with a dealer's invoice of $19,467. The GS was priced at $22,130 with a dealer's invoice of $18,991. Ford is not likely to tamper — not much, anyway — with the prices of these bread-and-butter biggies in 1994. Equipment and other changes for the new model year are minor.

Companion car: Only styling separates the Grand Marquis from the Ford Crown Victoria, a car bought by police departments nationwide. In addition to the improved side-impact barrier protection going into the Grand Marquis for 1994, the Crown Vic also gets dual air bags (already in the Marquis) and environmentally friendly air conditioner refrigerant.

Hometown: The Grand Marquis and Crown Vic are assembled in St. Thomas, Ontario.

OLDSMOBILE Eighty Eight Royale LS

With a note on the Buick LeSabre

When Yankees would ask us why we did this and that, a lot of us Southerners, black and white, would say: "We like it that way."

Even if we didn't like it — and most assuredly, some of us didn't — we'd say, "We like it that way." It was our way of saying, "Mind your own business until we're ready to change what we want to change."

And when change came, hallelujah! It didn't have to be major. If it was regarded as pleasant difference, it was cause enough for celebration, much like the hoopla going on at Oldsmobile nowadays.

Oldsmobile, the most traditional of General Motors Corp.'s product divisions, has given us the quintessential Southern car — the Eighty Eight Royale — a work of continuous improvement and modest alterations that has been revised again for 1994.

The new Eighty Eight Royale comes with dual air bags as standard equipment, and with optional brake-and-engine traction control. That's the serious stuff. But, frankly, serious engineering was never much of a

Praise: A perfect family mobile

Head-turning Quotient: Motorized Southern comfort

Ride, acceleration, handling: Triple aces

Brakes: Excellent

Suggested Retail Price: $20,000 - $24,000

U.S. Content: 90%

A perfect family mobile — great for long trips.

problem at Oldsmobile. Styling was.

Particularly, interior styling.

A failure of Southern life has been its tendency to embrace dowdiness as righteousness; and, God knows, the interiors of previous Oldsmobiles, with their tufted seats and linear dashboards, were righteous to the max.

The Eighty Eight Royale had fallen victim to glorified dowdiness, traces of which remain in the very name of the car — Eighty Eight Royale. Royale? Royale what? It sounds like a word from one of those "ancestry" conversations that fill the parlor rooms of some gene-conscious Southern families.

But, thankfully, the new Eighty Eight Royale's interior shows signs of breaking with that tradition. There's even a hint of sensuality in the reworked, rounded instrument panel, the smoothly revised interior door trim, and new leather trim option for seats. The interior now matches the car exterior, which was redesigned and modernized for 1992.

Revolutionary? Not by any stretch of the imagination. But it's progress, and welcome progress at that.

Background: The Oldsmobile Eighty Eight was introduced as a full-size, rear-wheel drive family car in 1949. It was converted to front-wheel drive in 1986. The car was reworked for 1992; but those changes, like many of the changes for 1994, were meant to polish the status quo. A modest mission. A mission accomplished.

There are three Eighty Eight models — the base Royale, the upscale Royale LS, and the Eighty Eight LSS (luxury sport sedan). All models are equipped with General Motors Corp.'s 3.8-liter V-6, rated 170 horsepower at 4,800 rpm with a maximum torque of 225 foot-pounds 3,200 rpm. A four-speed automatic transmission is standard in all Eighty Eights.

Complaints: My chief complaints about the 1992 Eighty Eight Royale concerned the dowdiness of the car's interior and the nonsensical location of the front air/heating vents at the bottom of the dashboard. Those matters have been corrected in the 1994 car.

Praise: The tested Eighty Eight Royale LS is a perfect family mobile, a wonderful road car — great for long trips. Its four-speed automatic transmission rivals that of the best big European luxury sedans. Overall construction is excellent.

Head-turning quotient: A more naughty front end for 1994. But the car is still motorized Southern comfort on Saturday and churchyard stuff come Sunday morning.

Ride, acceleration and handling: Triple aces, better in all three categories than some more expensive cars. Brakes — vented power front disc/rear drum with standard anti-lock backup — are excellent.

Mileage: About 23 to the gallon (18-gallon tank, estimated 400-mile range on usable volume of regular unleaded), running mostly highway and

Oldsmobile Eighty Eight Royale LS

driver only.

Sound system: Am/FM stereo radio and cassette, GM/Delco. Excellent.

Price note: Even with the equipment changes and styling upgrades, the 1994 Eight Royale will remain a "best-value," big-car buy with prices ranging from $20,000 to $24,000. Also, Oldsmobile dealers are willing to bargain on this one.

Companion cars: The Oldsmobile Eighty Eight Royale shares the same platform as the Buick LeSabre — and the Pontiac Bonneville. But the sporting Bonneville, particularly the SSE version, is sufficiently different in terms of demeanor and overall presentation to deserve separate treatment in this volume.

But the Eighty Eight and LeSabre are soulmates, as well as mechanical twins, although the LeSabre is a bit more stylistically hip than its Oldsmobile sibling. For 1994, the LeSabre also gets dual air bags and optional traction control.

Hometown: The Eighty Eight and Le Sabre are assembled in Flint, Mich.

PONTIAC Bonneville SSE

Complaints: Some people find the style pretentious

Praise: I like the styling. Sassy

Head-turning Quotient: Regenerates that flagging mid-life libido

Ride, Acceleration, Handling: Overall excellence

Brakes: Okay, but needs four-wheel discs with ABS

Suggested Retail Price: $25,000

Mileage: About 24 MPG

U.S. Content: 90%

By the end of the New York-to-Washington run, the "bright white primary" paint on the Pontiac SSE had turned dingy brown, accented by green streaks from flying windshield-wiper fluid. The car looked a mess, having been driven through a storm. But I patted its metal anyway upon disembarking. It was the least I could do for an automobile that pulled me through so much so well with style.

Dirty or not, the SSE was a sexy machine with its ribbed and rounded body, its feline headlamps and flared rear. It had a wildness about it that carried over into the passenger cabin, with its lava-flow instrument panel that, remarkably, positioned all dials and gauges, including a video compass, exactly where they were needed.

More notable was the absence of dated gimcrackery that General Motors Corp. once routinely stuck in its cars. These items included coffin handles on interior door panels, totally fake woodgrain and bawdy-house velour, all of which was missing from the passenger cabin of the SSE.

What was there was mostly good stuff, well-assembled and tightly stitched. Even the composition of the interior door panels — quality molded vinyl with carpet inlays at the bottom and, yes, functional handles — bespoke a kind of design consistency that GM, at long last, seems to be turning into a habit.

Mechanically, the SSE was a match for any other full-size, luxury sports sedan on the turnpike. It sent road-spray flying into a good number of Acura and Lexus windshields, and even splattered a 5-series BMW or two. And, thanks to its suck-the-road, 16-inch Goodyear Eagle GT+4 tires and its four-wheel independent suspension system, the SSE stayed on the highway in spots where other cars slipped and swerved.

All things considered, maybe patting the SSE's metal wasn't a good enough "Thank you." I should've kissed it, or hugged it, or something.

Background: The SSE is part of the Pontiac Bonneville family; but the Pontiac people are hiding the Bonneville name on this one. It's a class thing. The SSE appeals to affluent, import-oriented buyers who regard the Bonneville nameplate as a dorky throwback to 1950s, small-town America.

However, the base SE is more enthusiastically linked to the Bonneville name in Pontiac marketing. That's because buyers of those models — mostly college-educated men, age 47, with household incomes of $67,000 — are modest folks who like the idea of driving a Bonneville, according to Pontiac's market research.

Buyers of the SSE, on the other hand, are more, uhm, cosmopolitan. The average SSE buyer is a college-educated man in his mid-40s with a

Pontiac Bonneville SSE

household income of $93,000 to $123,000.

Both Bonneville models, the only two on sale for 1994, are front-wheel-drive, six-passenger cars.

For 1994, the base Bonnevile engine is a fuel-injected, 3.8-liter V-6 rated 170 horsepower at 4,800 rpm. Maximum torque is 225 footpounds at 3,200 rpm. That engine is standard on the SE and SSE.

The tested SSE was GM's optional, supercharged 3.8-liter V-6, the same engine used in the 1994 Buick Park Avenue Ultra. The optional engine is rated 225 horsepower at 5,000 rpm with a maximum torque of 275 foot-pounds at 3,200 rpm. The new engine has 20 more horsepower than the comparable powerplant in the 1993 SSE.

An electronically controlled, four-speed automatic transmission is standard on the SE and SSE. Also standard for 1994 are dual air bags and power, four-wheel front disc/rear drum brakes with anti-lock backup.

Complaints: My complaint about the 1993 Bonneville SSE was that the engine noise, deliberately growly, needed to be toned down. Pontiac since has discovered that some people don't like to hear their motors run, and has reduced the engine-decibel level in the 1994 car. Thanks, Pontiac. You really do care.

However, the SSE's aggressive styling is still a turn-off to some people, including some men, who find it pretentious.

Praise: I like the styling. It's hip, flip, more fun than the trip. Given its overall quality, construction and sassiness, the SSE is one hot-to-trot car, easily competitive with most cars in the performance-luxury category.

Head-turning quotient: A motorized regenerative for flagging mid-life libidos, a hit among members of the Second Childhood League.

Ride, acceleration and handling: Overall excellence. The qualifier is needed because the SSE ought to come with four-wheel-disc brakes, instead of the standard front discs/rear drums. The car stops okay with the standard setup. But four-wheel-discs along with standard ABS brakes could improve that performance.

Mileage: In the 1994 SSE with the supercharged 3.8-liter V-6, about 24 to the gallon (18-gallon tank, estimated 420-mile range on usable volume of required premium unleaded). Running mostly highway and driver only.

Sound system: Optional eight-speaker AM/FM stereo radio and cassette with graphic equalizer, the new Delco 2001 Series. Oh, yes! Get on up!

Price: Pontiac streamlined the Bonneville line in 1994, dropping the SSEi, which sold at a base price of $29,444. But many SSEi features have either been made standard, or made available as options for the SSE, which sold for about $25,000 in 1993. The upshot is higher prices, but more content for the SSE in 1994. Bottom line: In the new model year, the Bonneville price spread will range form near $20,000 for the base Bonneville SE to near $30,000 for the SSE equipped with the supercharged V-6.

Hometown: The Bonneville SE and SSE are assembled in Lake Orion, Mich.

5

Too Hot To Handle

Super American Sports Machines — Money's No Object

CHEVROLET Corvette ZR-1 Coupe

It was an old lover with old habits, and it didn't matter that it was wrapped in new clothing. It ran the same, which is to say, it ran wild, with more muscle than sophistication. And that was odd, because the car was loaded with technology.

It was the Chevrolet Corvette, of course — a car that changes all the while it resists change. It's an art that the Corvette has mastered in its 40th production year, as evidenced by the 1994 model.

The interior is redone in the new Corvette. There are dual air bags, finally. And the instrument panel, with its day-white, night-tangerine graphics — it changes color when the sun goes off and the headlamps come on — makes sense.

The seats are new, too. At least, General Motors sez so. I'm skeptical because the new seats felt the same as the old ones, which wasn't so bad. The old seats were comfortable.

There is new carpeting in the car and a new, two-spoke steering wheel, and interior door panels that have some practical use. Pockets are now in the panels. You can put things in those places.

Ah, and there's the "express down" driver's window — press a button

Complaints: Overpowered	
Praise: What's love got to do with it?	
Head-turning Quotient: 405-horsepower Tina Turner	
Ride, Acceleration, Handling: Phenomenally good, however it's a butt-buster	
Brakes: Excellent	
Suggested Retail Price: $34,595 - $ 41,195	
Mileage: About 21 MPG	
U.S. Content: 95%	

*Future Corvettes
will be smaller,
more lightweight,
and more fuel-
efficient.*

and the window goes all the way down automatically, which isn't really new technology; but it's new to the Corvette.

You sense some lethargy in these words, a kind of "so what?" Well, it's not that, not really.

I've known and loved the Corvette for a long time. But now, it seems older, incapable of changing for the better. It still offers the same old thrills, yes. Va-va-voooom and all of that. But it doesn't seem to be about much more, which is too bad.

There are other cars out there that can, and do, run faster than the Corvette. But they do it with a sophistication, an ease that escapes my thunderous friend, which — depending on whether you buy it as a coupe, convertible, or ZR-1 — weighs anywhere from 3,317 pounds to 3,358 pounds.

It's time for a change; and as much as I love the Corvette, I've gotta say it's behind the times.

For example, the new ZR-1 I drove was a hot runner; but it was too hot for local driving conditions, too hot anywhere except on back roads leading to nowhere in particular. And the car literally growled its way through daily commutes, almost as if it resented those low-speed trips. All it wanted to do was run.

But sports cars nowadays have to be about more than being fast. They've got to offer some kind of balance between excitement and common sense. The current Corvette doesn't.

Background: Corvette sales fell from 30,424 in 1985 to 19,819 in 1992; and by the middle of calendar 1993, signs were that the car's sales would fall even lower.

It's time for a change, and the change has to be more than cosmetic, more than tweakings of already way-too-powerful engines.

The word out of Detroit is that General Motors has just such changes in mind for the 1996 Corvette, which could come with V-6's well as the V-8's. And the future Corvettes will be smaller, more lightweight, and more fuel-efficient — and, believe it or not, more fun, those GM sources say.

Until then, buyers can choose from the extant fleet of fast and heavy Corvettes, available with two V-8 engines.

There is the standard 'Vette hummer — the LT1 V-8, rated 300-horsepower at 5,000 rpm with a maximum torque of 340 foot-pounds at 3,600 rpm. And then there's the LT5 V-8, found in the Corvette Extremus, also known as the ZR-1.

The LT5 engine is rate 405 horsepower at 5,800 rpm, with a maximum torque of 385 foot-pounds at 5,200 rpm.

The LT1 engine is mated with a standard four-speed automatic transmission, the electronically controlled 4L60-E model. The ZR-1 gets a standard six-speed manual transmission.

Chevrolet Corvette ZR-1

Standard brakes include power four-wheel-discs with anti-lock back-up.

Corvettes are front-engine, rear-drive two-seaters.

Complaints: Enough said.

Praise: I love the ZR-1. But, what's love got to do with it?

Head-turning quotient: Tina Turner with a 405-horsepower engine and six-speed rhythm. We all know that Tina's getting up in age, lasting longer than she should've lasted. Ditto the Corvette. But both car and star are still stunningly beautiful and sexy as hell.

Ride, acceleration, handling: The Corvette ZR-1 ride remains something of a butt-buster. Handling and acceleration are phenomenally good. Braking — Thank God! — is excellent.

Mileage: About 21 to the gallon (20-gallon tank, estimated 408-mile range on usable volume of premium unleaded), combined city-highway, running driver only with light cargo.

Price note: The Chevrolet Corvette closed the 1993-model year with retail prices ranging from $34,595 to $41,195. Dealer invoice prices ranged from $29,579 to $35,222. Expect some price increases to cover 1994 equipment changes. But, hey, Chevrolet isn't exactly setting the world on fire with Corvette sales. You can bargain.

Hometown: The Corvette is made in Bowling Green, Ky.

Complaints: No air conditioner, no air bags, hot side exhaust pipes

Praise: Whhhooossshhh!

Head-turning Quotient: Zeeeooowww!

Ride, Acceleration, Handling: Zeeeooowww!

Brakes: Excellent

Suggested Retail Price: $60,000 - $70,000

Mileage: About 14 MPG

U.S. Content: 90%

DODGE Viper RT/10

Two hours of my date with the snake were spent in a garage waiting for the rain to stop. In any other car, it would've been an intolerable waste of time. Heck, in another car, I could've gone out in the rain. But the snake, the Dodge Viper RT/10, was no ordinary car.

It was a topless vibration, pure sex. No other way to put it. And it was red, very red, with a low-down, muscular, round body that could've come from the Priapus School of Design. It proved beyond a reasonable doubt that sex sells.

People just wouldn't leave the Viper alone; they were all over the thing, cooing, mooing, stroking, touching. It was embarrassing. In the two days that I had the car, I got more propositions than I received in 45 years of living, which was both exciting and depressing when I thought about it.

Anyway, I sat there in the garage, answering folks' questions about the Viper, laughing, smiling and cursing myself for not attaching the Viper's fairly worthless, fabric-and-vinyl roof and its attendant sidescreens. But the day began with sunshine, bright and beautiful. I just couldn't bring myself to do the roof thing. I hopped in the Viper and took the longest possible route to the office, arriving nearly two hours late.

That night, I headed for Baltimore with a Viper-smitten colleague, but had to dump my chum at the train station when storm clouds threatened. The downpour began before I could exit the station's multi-deck garage. And there I sat, imprisoned by the elements and the beautiful, motorized beast. Oh, what splendid incarceration!

Background: There are fools and dreamers and, thankfully, Chrysler Corp., the Viper's maker, has lots of both. Fools are needed to challenge the mediocrity of convention. To wit: they must be "foolish" enough to try something considered impossible or unwise by everyone else. Dreamers are needed to give color and shape to vision, to give it poetry and romance. Those are the kind of people who worked on the original Team Viper, all 80 of 'em, a bunch of gearheads, nuts, poets and engineers led by Chrysler President Robert Lutz, racing great Carroll Shelby, and executive engineer Roy Sjoberg.

Dodge Viper RT/10

Shelby created the original snake cars, the Shelby Cobra models, in another lifetime when he was affiliated with Ford Motor Co. Clearly, the Chrysler people were deep into Cobra-think nearly five years ago when they conceived the Viper. They wanted to create a basic, high-performance, front-engine, rear-wheel-drive, two-passenger, two-door roadster with tremendous eye appeal. They succeeded.

Complaints: Anything as impractical as the Viper is bound to have problems, and the Viper has plenty. There is no air conditioner, which means you can hardly breathe inside the Viper on hot, rainy days when the top and sidescreens are in place. There are no outside door handles and no air bags, either. The side-mounted exhaust pipes get hot and, despite being insulated, they stay hot enough long enough to singe you if you are not getting out of the car. And, yes, the Viper is the noisiest reptile on Earth.

And the Viper has other problems:

Chrysler built 700 Vipers in 1993, some 2,000 less than needed to fill car orders that model year. The company plans to build 1,000 Vipers in the 1994-model year, about 3,000 short of the mark needed to fill pending and expected orders.

Why the slow-down? Chrysler is having trouble getting composite plastic hoods to fit properly on the Viper. Until the problem is worked out, it's moving painstakingly slowly in producing the car.

Praise: The Viper is not meant to be practical. It is a fair-weather roadster designed primarily to entertain driver and spectator. The car does a marvelous job of doing both. There is nothing — repeat, nothing like cranking up that big, eight-liter, 400-horsepower, V-10 engine and letting it rip! Sinful? You betcha. Fun? Definitely. Four-hundred horsepower at 4,600 rpm, with a maximum torque of 462 foot-pounds at 3,600 rpm! Whh-hooossshhh! It's the perfect antidote for those who have attended too many celebrations of the death of passion.

Head-turning quotient: Zeeeeooowww!

Ride, acceleration and handling: Zeeeeooowww! It gets a little bumpy on bad roads, but who cares? That V-10 has so much twisting power, you can launch yourself into oblivion in almost any of the Viper's six gears. Brakes include vented, power-assisted discs front and rear. And those tires — yipes! Big, 17-inch-diameter huggamuggas that really stick to the road.

Sound system: Get outta here! I should listen to the radio in this car? Nahhh! With all of the engine and wind noise, I probably would not have heard anything anyway.

Mileage: Horrendous! About 14 miles per gallon (20-gallon tank, estimated 275-mile range on usable volume of premium unleaded gasoline), running mostly highway with one to two occupants.

Price note: Ha! How much you wanna pay? Fifty-thousand dollars? Get outta here! Sixty-thousand? Ahhh, maybe we'll talk. Seventy-thousand? Okay, you sound serious. Let's talk.

In terms of retail, there is nothing about the Viper that's fixed price.

Hometown: Deeeetroittt! The Viper is assembled at Chrysler's Mack Avenue Plant in the Motor City.

6

Long-Haul Lovin'

Pickup Trucks

DODGE Dakota Club Cab Pickup

Pretty colors and pickup trucks. I suppose I'll get used to them. Although, it seems wasteful to paint a truck "dark blue pearl-coat" and then drive the thing to a compost heap, which is where I took the new Dodge Dakota Club Cab pickup. I took it to a lumber yard and waste-disposal site, too, and to other places where one shouldn't take anything painted pearl-coat, dark blue.

And this was extremely light duty for the Dakota, a mid-size pickup that once would've been more at home on the farm and at construction sites than in suburban driveways, landfills, and shopping-mall parking lots.

But trucks, even pickups, aren't what they used to be — exclusive beasts of burden primarily designed to carry cargo, and a few people who didn't mind being bumped along.

Today's trucks, as evidenced by the Dakota and a myriad of other models, are more civilized. That is not to say that they've become "cars," as some people might suggest.

No, they remain very much trucks; but with some acknowledgement that people, too, have needs, including the need for beauty — for pretty

Complaints: Sideview mirrors too large, poor brakes	
Praise: Tough, rugged, well-constructed	
Ride, Acceleration, Handling: Rides like a truck, runs like truck, feels like a truck	
Brakes: Unimpressive	
Suggested Retail Price: $9,154 - $16,240	
Mileage: About 16 MPG	
U.S. Content: 97%	

Parties as well as

it works.

paint and pretty interiors, such as the tested Dakota's mix of light wood-grains and soft blues, and its deep-piled carpet.

All of this pretty stuff makes for a lot of cleanup work after a few trips to the compost heap. But the payoff comes after the hauling and cleaning's been done, when both you and the truck have been spruced up and made ready to party.

Background: The tested four-wheel-drive Club Cab is the top of the Dakota pickup line, which includes two-wheel and four-wheel-drive models.

The Club Cab seats six people. The Dakota Standard Cab pickup seats three. Both versions are available in four trim levels — Base, Work, Sport, and Sport Luxury Truck (SLT).

For 1994, the Dakota gets a standard driver's air bag, actually a "face bag," which has a somewhat smaller deployment area than drivers' bags in passenger cars. A new knee bolster, to help prevent "submarining" — sliding under the dashboard — also is standard in the 1994 Dakota.

Other 1994 changes include steel side-door beams for improved side-impact crash protection; improved roll-over roof-crush protection, and the use of R-134a air-conditioner refrigerant, which environmentalists claim to be harmless to the earth's ozone layer.

The standard engine in the two-wheel-drive, Standard Cab Dakota models is a 2.5-liter, four-cylinder, electronically fuel-injected job rated 99 horsepower at 4,500 rpm. Maximum torque is 132 foot-pounds at 2,800 rpm.

All Club Cabs and four-wheel-drive Dakotas get a standard 3.9-liter V-6 capable of producing 175 horsepower at 4,800 rpm. Maximum torque is 225 foot-pounds at 3,200 rpm.

Optional equipment includes a 5.2 liter, fuel-injected V-8 rated 220 horsepower at 4,400 rpm. Maximum torque is 295 foot-pounds at 3,200 rpm.

The Dakota trucks can be outfitted with five-speed manual or four-speed automatic transmissions.

Brakes include standard, vented front discs and rear drums with a rear anti-lock brake system.

Standard cargo bed is 6.5 feet; a bed eight-feet long is available. The Dakota trucks can be equipped to carry payloads ranging from 1,250 lbs. to 2,800 lbs.

Complaints: Some elements of ergonomic goofiness — a remote-control lever for the sideview mirrors that is center-left on the dashboard, exactly where the headlamp switch should be; a head-lamp switch located lower-left on the instrument panel, exactly where the mirror-control lever should be; sideview mirrors so large, they can block your view of *oncoming* traffic.

Dodge Dakota Club Cab

Ah, yes. Add unimpressive braking. The tested Dakota Club Cab tended to roll — that's roll, not slide or skid — some seven to 10 feet *after* brakes were applied.

Praise: An overall, well-constructed pickup truck. Tough, rugged; but it parties as well as it works. Hats off to Chrysler Corp. for putting a driver's bag in the 1994 model.

Ride, acceleration, handling: Forget the pretty color and other happy stuff. The Dakota Club Cab rides, runs, and feels like a pickup truck — which is to say that human rumps will feel the bumps in this one, and that anyone trying to swing this truck around a sharp curve is something less than intelligent.

The test truck was equipped with the optional 5.2-liter V-8. It roared!

Mileage: About 16 to the gallon (optional 22-gallon tank, estimated 340-mile range on usable volume of regular unleaded), combine city-highway, running with one to three occupants and cargo loads ranging from 200 lbs. to 850 lbs.

A 15-gallon fuel tank is standard.

Sound system: Optional four-speaker, electronic AM/FM stereo radio and cassette with graphic equalizer, Infinity system. Very nice.

Price: Dakota trucks ended the 1993-model year with base prices ranging from $9,154 to $16,240. Dealer invoices on those models ranged from $8,777 to $14,686. Expect moderate price increases in 1994. (That air bag, after all, does not come free of charge.) But Chrysler dealers want to move the Dakotas. They're willing to bargain.

Hometown: Dodge Dakota trucks are assembled in "Dodge City," Warren, Mich.

DODGE Ram Pickup

Complaints: None, yet
Praise: That styling! And a smooth ride too
Head-turning Quotient: Yessir!
Ride, Acceleration, Handling: All good. Very smooth
Brakes: Excellent
Suggested Retail Price: Around $16,000
Mileage: About 16 MPG
U.S. Content: 91%

This is the daddy of all pickups, the biggest of the big, the baddest of the bad. That's "bad" as in hip, flip, hell of a ship. The 1994 Dodge Ram pickup. There is no other pickup like it, which ain't hyperbole.

Take a look at that front end. Good golly, Miss Molly! Have you ever anywhere in your whole life seen a pickup truck that looked like that? Long, protruding hood flanked by flared fenders with flush headlamps. Big chrome grille — big, big chrome grille with four slits, each with a wire-mesh backing, and a don't-mess-with-me ram's-head insignia in the center of it all.

Hell, I'd buy it for the looks alone; and I'd get it in "flame red," one of 10 colors available for the 1994 Ram pickups. And I'd get it with polished stainless steel wheels and bright hub caps to really show off that hot red paint. Yes!

Do I love this truck! You betcha! It's so in-your-face, so kiss-my-assets, so up-your-nose-with-a-rubber-hose. Adolescent? Probably. I dunno, and could care less. All I know is that I love it! A pickup with an attitude — nasty and nice. And you know what? The darned thing works pretty good, too.

Background: The 1994 Dodge Ram pickup is what happens when an auto maker allows its designers and engineers to be designers and engineers, when it allows them to cut loose, let go, and use their imaginations.

Not everybody will like the results. Big whoop. Anything or anyone in aggressive pursuit of individuality will turn off someone; and, surely, a number of people will be turned off by the new Ram pickup.

But here's wagering that more of us will be turned on by this bold, fresh departure from traditional pickup design, this no-compromise breaking of the rules.

Dodge Ram Pickup

Here's betting, too, that many people with misgivings about the Ram pickup's styling will be won over by the common sense of the thing. To wit: the bodaciously large standard cabin, the largest in the industry with 40.2 inches of headroom, 41 inches legroom, 66.3 inches shoulder room, 65.8 inches for hips. You can seat three big people comfortably in the Ram pickup. And, hey, you can put those seats in a reclining position when you want to catch some zzz's at a rest stop.

Personal items, such as small overnight bags, can be carried in the cabin, which also has lots of storage space. Not many standard pickups offer that service.

Safety? A driver's air bag (face type) is standard, along with steel door beams to help protect occupants in side-impact crashes. Roll-over roof-crush protection, enhanced by a full roof inner panel, is best in class. Rear-wheel anti-lock brakes are standard.

Five engines are available, including a 3.9-liter V-6, 5.2-liter V-8, 5.9-liter V-8, 5.9-liter inline-six diesel, and an 8-liter gasoline V-10.

The 3.9-liter V-6 — 175 horsepower at 4,800 rpm, maximum torque of 230 foot-pounds at 3,200 rpm — is standard on the half-ton, two-wheel-drive Ram 1500 pickup. The 5.2-liter V-8 — 220 horsepower at 4,400 rpm, maximum torque of 300 foot-pounds at 3,200 rpm — is standard on the three-quarter-ton Ram 2500 pickup in two-wheel-drive and four-wheel-drive.

The Ram 3500, with standard dual rear-wheels, gets the heavy-duty 5.9-liter V-8 rated 230 horsepower at 4,000 rpm with a maximum torque of 330 foot-pounds at 2,800 rpm.

Optional engines include the 8-liter V-10 and the 5.9-liter, inline six-cylinder diesel rated 175 horsepower at 2,500 rpm, with a maximum torque of 420 foot-pounds at 1,600 rpm.

The big hugga-mugga, the V-10, is rated 300 horsepower at 4,000 rpm with a maximum torque of 450 foot-pounds at 2,400 rpm. That engine becomes available in January 1994, six months before Chrysler begins producing Club Cab versions of its new Ram pickup.

Ram cargo-box sizes range from 6.5 feet to eight feet. The pickups can be outfitted to carry payloads ranging from 1,787 lbs. to 5,288 lbs.

Ram pickup trim packages include the Work Special, Base, sporty ST, and the top-line Laramie SLT. The Rams are available with five-speed manual and four-speed automatic transmissions.

Complaints: None — yet.

Praise: Look, I'm wacko over the styling of the thing — maybe, too wacko. But, as indicated earlier, the new Ram pickups have lots of substantial stuff to go along with the looks. Other goodies include one-piece cargo box made of high-strength steel, indentations in the cargo-box sides designed to hold 2x8 lumber, 16-inch tires, and front-rear suspension systems that give this tough truck a smooth ride.

Head-turning quotient: Eeeeowwww! Yessir! What the hell is *that?!* Gets attention everywhere it goes.

Ride, acceleration and handling: Unbelievably smooth for a full-size pickup truck. The briefly tested standard Ram 1500, two-wheel-drive, came with an independent front suspension that allowed eight inches of suspension travel — up-and-down motion — for a surprisingly comfortable ride. Handling was excellent, but still discernably the handling of a truck, which means you don't swing this one around sharp curves, either.

Acceleration was excellent. The Ram 1500 was equipped with a standard 3.9-liter V-6 and a five-speed manual transmission.

Braking, mercifully, was good. (Mercifully, because a reporter for a Detroit newspaper got ahold of a prototype 1994 Ram pickup in which the brakes failed.) Standard brakes include power, vented front discs/rear drums with a rear anti-lock system.

Mileage: In the tested Ram 1500, estimated 16 miles per gallon (26-gallon tank, estimated 400-mile range on usable volume of regular unleaded), running mostly highway and driver only.

Sound system: Not much. Standard two-speaker, electronically controlled AM/FM "stereo" radio. Boring as hell.

If you buy the Ram pickup, treat yourself to something nice — the optional four-speaker, electronically controlled AM/FM stereo radio and cassette Dolby sound. And if you're really an audiophile, go for the absolutely wonderful, six-speaker Infinity system.

Price note: Retail prices on the 1993 Dodge Ram pickups ranged from $8,865 to $24,657, with dealer invoice prices running from $8,475 to $21,428. Unless Chrysler feels rich enough to give away money, 1994 Ram pickup prices will come in substantially higher to help cover the costs of redesign and new equipment. Still, buyers will be able to get a well-contented, 1994 Ram pickup for about $16,000 or so.

Hometown: The Dodge Ram pickups are assembled at — where else? — "Dodge City" in Warren, Mich.

FORD Ranger XLT Compact Pickup

With Notes on Mazda's 1994 B-Series Compact Pickup

The pickup truck came with chilly fall weather, and I considered using it to haul away bags of leaves and other organic rubbish. But that idea was nixed by our resident environmentalist, who suggested that the leaves be mulched and spread along the perimeter of the back yard in some seasonal ceremony of last rites.

So there was little to do except drive the truck, a new Ford Ranger XLT 4x4, a thing of electric red paint and rounded features. I headed for Virginia's Shenandoah Valley in search of real people.

Real people are those who have some actual use for pickups and, thus, some reasoned appreciation of their value. They are no-nonsense folks who call 'em as they see 'em; and what they saw in the new Ranger XLT 4x4 was, as one man put it, "one damn fine truck."

The man said he had lots of experience with Ford trucks; and then he made me an offer I easily refused. He pointed to his blue Ford F-150 pickup, a circa 1988 job that had more than its share of dents and scratches, and a pretty cruddy-looking cabin to boot.

"Trade ya," he said.

I laughed. He laughed. We said goodbye.

Background: More than 3 million Ford Ranger trucks have been sold since the pickup's introduction in 1982 as a 1983 model. That makes the Ranger the best-selling compact pickup in the United States.

With Ford's dominance of the compact pickup segment, it was easy to assume that the company would motor along with its formerly square, sturdy Rangers, content to rake in a tidy profit on every Ranger sold. But

Complaints: Cramped interior

Praise: Generally well-done. Good 4WD system

Head-turning Quotient: A hit

Ride, Acceleration, Handling: Improved handling

Suggested Retail Price: $8,631 - $16,585

Mileage: About 16 MPG

U.S. Content: 88%

Ford Ranger Splash SuperCab — 1994

Ford had a better idea.

The company did a major overhaul of the Ranger in 1993, redoing the exterior sheetmetal, installing flush glass and limo-style doors, spiffing up the once-dowdy and ergonomically inept instrument panel, and restyling the seats. And just for fun, Ford introduced the super-wild, flared-rear, "Splash" version of the Ranger in mid-1993.

The 1994 Ranger, as a result, gets only a few changes. Chief among those are side-door beams to help increase occupant safety in side-impact crashes and, ahmm, cargo box tie-down hooks. There's also a SuperCab version of the standard cab Splash Ranger in the works.

And then, there's this: the Mazda Ranger, which won't be called a Ranger. It's coming to market in 1994 as the Mazda B-Series pickup .

Other than its nameplate and a few stylistic changes, the Mazda pick-up practically will be identical to the Ranger, on which it is based. Ford will build both vehicles.

The Ranger is available in five trim levels, the base XL, XL Sport, flared-box Ranger Splash, luxury Ranger XLT and the super-spiffy Ranger STX. All Rangers are available in two-wheel and four-wheel drive.

The Ranger is equipped with a standard fuel-injected, 2.3-liter, inline four-cylinder engine rated 100 horsepower at 4,600 rpm. Maximum torque is 133 foot-pounds at 2,600 rpm. A five-speed manual transmission is standard. A four-speed automatic overdrive transmission is optional.

Optional engines include a 3-liter and 4-liter V-6, both of which can be linked to five-speed manual or four-speed automatic transmissions. The 3-liter V-6 is rated 145 horsepower at 4,800 rpm with a maximum torque of 165 foot-pounds at 3,000 rpm.

When coupled with a five-speed manual overdrive, the 4-liter V-6 is rated 145 horsepower at 3,800 rpm with a maximum torque of 220 foot-pounds at 2,400 rpm. When connected to a four-speed automatic, the 4-liter V-6 is designed to deliver 160 horsepower at 4,200 rpm with a maximum torque of 230 foot-pounds at 2,400 rpm.

Standard brakes include power front discs/rear drums with a rear anti-lock system.

Payload capacity: The Ranger can be equipped to carry cargo payloads up to 1,650 lbs. The Ranger's short cargo box is six-feet long. The long box is seven feet.

Complaints: Cramped space in the Regular Cab Ranger, especially cramped for anyone long of leg or wide of girth. But short people also have some gripes with this one. They complain that the absence of interior, roof-mounted hand grips makes it difficult for them to pull themselves into the Ranger XLT 4x4's cabin.

Also, illuminated instrument-panel glare on the rear window is a pain.

Praise: Generally well-done redesign, including the suspension refinements that give the new Rangers a more car-like ride. Excellent overall construction in the tested XLT 4x4. Also, the automatic, push-button, four-wheel-drive system works perfectly.

Head-turning quotient: A hit among current Ranger owners and owners of compact, Japanese-made pickups.

Ride, acceleration and handling: There's a little less truckiness in the ride of the new Ranger XLT 4x4, Handling has improved, partly thanks to the truck's wider track. But, hey, it's still a truck. You can't do curves in this one the way you can do them in cars.

Mileage: In the tested 1993 XLT 4x4 (same specs as the 1994 model), about 16 miles per gallon (16.3-gallon tank, estimated 250-mile range on usable volume of regular unleaded), running mostly highway with one to two occupants and light cargo.

Sound system: Four-speaker AM/FM stereo radio and cassette. Ford installed. Very good.

Price note: Ranger prices ranged from $8,631 to $16,585 at the close of the 1993-model year. Dealer invoice prices stretched from $8,046 to $14,701. Expect a slight rise in 1994 prices to cover modest product changes. But most Ford dealers have always been willing to bargain on Rangers.

Please note that there is not one reason to pay more for a comparably

A hit among current Ranger owners and owners of compact, Japanese-made pickups.

equipped, 1994 Mazda B-series pickup, or vice versa if there's a higher price on the Ranger. The trucks are identical.

Hometowns: Ford Rangers are made in Louisville, Ky., Twin Cities, Minn., and Edison, N.J. The Mazda B-Series pickup will be assembled in Edison.

Complaints: No air bags
Praise: At the top of the list for small pickups
Ride, Acceleration, Handling: Excellent
Suggested Retail Price: $9,806 - $16,613
Mileage: About 23 MPG
U.S. Content: 95%

GMC Truck Sonoma

With Notes on the Chevrolet S-Series Pickup

The somnolent Sonoma is somnolent no more.

GMC's sleepy little pickup got a wake-up call for 1994; and it's spry, sly, and ready to fly!

Check the scope:

The truck's jive-time boxiness has been jettisoned in favor of sassy curves, front and rear. Even the tailgate — a curved piece wedged between two flippant taillamps — looks good.

The old truck's silly instrument panel, which looked like something you'd hang over a baby's crib, has been replaced. The new panel is attractive, adult, and ergonomically correct with large, easy-to-use controls. A legible analog display now tells you exactly what you need to know about the truck's operation.

Interior space in the new Sonoma is actually decent. In the previous truck, the only reason you stayed awake on long trips was because you were too cramped and beaten to doze off.

And the engine noise! Lord! Where did that go? Sometimes, after a trip of 100 miles or so, you'd climb out of the old Sonoma, and your head would be buzzin'.

But the new Sonoma is mercifully quiet, thanks to the generous use of sound-deadening materials and the judicious placement of seals, such as those located at the rear edges of the truck's doors.

Ah, and the seats! Whoever designed the Sonoma's new seats must have a behind that's over 45 years old. The old seats disrespected aging butts by being firm in all the wrong places. The new seats are more friendly to the lower back, kinder to the spreading rump.

What's going on here?

Methinks the folks at General Motors finally realized that most people buy small pickups for personal use — maybe because they can't, or don't want to spend more money on a car. Methinks, too, GM's designers and

GMC Truck Sonoma

engineers finally heard the noise outside their studio and office windows — the whoosh of people rushing to buy smartly styled, well-engineered Ford Ranger and Toyota SR5 compact trucks.

Whatever the case, we should be grateful. In the 1994 Sonoma and its practically identical twin, the Chevrolet S-Series pickup, we now have two GM compact trucks that prove "inexpensive" need not be brutal and "economy" need not be boring.

Background: GM's compact trucks were introduced in 1982 primarily as cheap commercial transportation — small trucks that could be used by small businesses in delivery, service and construction work. They were reliable, functional pieces, but not terribly sophisticated.

Still, partially because of recessions and changing demographics, these small trucks began to appeal to more and more personal-use buyers — people who simply wanted to use them to get around. Problem was, until recently, GM never got around to finding out who those people were.

Now, GM has done its homework, and the results are mostly impressive — the 1994 GMC Truck Sonoma and companion Chevrolet S-Series pickup — two trucks bound to give Ford and Toyota a run for the compact-truck money.

These trucks are all-new. Look at their engine bays, where you'll find a new, standard 2.2-liter, fuel-injected, inline four-cylinder engine rated 118-horsepower at 5,200 rpm with a maximum torque of 130 foot-pounds at

The Sonoma/S-series trucks move to the top of the list of small pickups, foreign and domestic, based on their overall quality, engineering and presentation. Good work, GM.

2,800 rpm. That's 13 more horsepower than was delivered by the 2.5-liter inline four in the 1993 Sonoma and S-Series pickups — more horsepower with less fuel-consumption, thanks to weight-saving steps taken in the engineering and design of the new engine.

The 2.2-liter four is mated with a standard five-speed manual transmission in two-wheel-drive Sonoma and S-Series trucks. A four-speed automatic is optional in that configuration.

Two 4.3-liter, V-6 engines are available. One, the L35 V-6, is rated 195 horsepower at 4,500 rpm with a maximum torque of 260 foot-pounds at 3,600 rpm. The other, the LB4 V-6, comes in at 165 horsepower at 4,000 rpm with a maximum torque of 235 foot-pounds at 2,400 rpm.

The LB4 V-6 is standard on four-wheel-drive Sonoma/S-Series pickups and optional on the two-wheel-drive models. The L35 V-6 is optional for both the four-wheel-drive and two-wheel-drive pickups. A four-speed automatic transmission is standard with the more powerful V-6. That transmission is optional with the LB4 engine.

Standard brakes include power front discs/rear drums. A rear-wheel anti-lock system is standard on two-wheel-drive models equipped with the 2.2-liter inline four engine. A four-wheel anti-lock system is standard on all Sonoma/S-Series pickups equipped with LB4 or L35 V-6 engines.

Body notes: The Sonoma and S-Series pickups are built on three wheelbases — the center-line distances between the front and rear wheels measured in inches. Those models include regular cab/short box (108.3 inches); regular cab/long box (117.9 inches); and extended cab, short box (122.9 inches).

The term "box" is used generically in describing the Sonoma/S-Series rear payload area; because they're so well-shaped, they aren't your traditional "boxes" at all. Let's call 'em cargo bays, the shortest of which stretches six feet, and the longest of which extends 7.5 feet. The cargo bays have pockets to hold boards that can be used to create a second-tier loading floor.

Interior cabin space widens by 1.8 inches over previous models. Shoulder room goes up three inches; head room up a smidgen, 0.3 inch, and hip room widens 0.7 inch. Add to that a greater use of glass — 30-percent more — and you get a compact-pickup cabin that's at least livable.

Oh, yes, the matter of side-impact crash protection — all Sonoma/S-Series pickups now come with side-door guard beams.

Tale of the seven sisters: suspension systems include all of the mechanical parts and structures needed to support the vehicle body above the wheels. Suspension systems largely determine the vehicle's ride quality, cornering ability and carrying capacity.

There are seven — yes, seven — pre-packaged suspension systems available in the 1994 Sonoma/S-Series pickup lines.

There are three packages for the two-wheel-drive pickups. Those include a "solid-smooth ride" suspension, "high payload" suspension, and "sport" suspension.

There are four packages for the four-wheel-drive pickups. Those include "solid-smooth ride" and "high payload," as well as an "off-road" suspension and a "highrider" suspension for even more rugged off-road use.

Figure out how you're going to use the truck — and pleeeeze be honest with yourself. None of that Walter Mitty stuff about truckin' off to the badlands over the weekend, when all you're gonna do is go to the shopping mall, come home and watch football. Order your suspension package accordingly. (Oh, bullcrap! You know danged well you ain't goin' whitewater raftin'. Better get off your butt, clean that yard, and haul that trash away.)

Towing, payload, seating capacities: The Sonoma/S-Series pickups can be outfitted to carry up to 1,567 lbs. of cargo and to pull a trailer weighing 6,000 lbs.

Regular cabs seat three people. Extended cabs seat five.

Complaints: It blows my mind that GM did all of this work to create two, splendid new compact pickups — without a single air bag. Unbelievable!

Praise: Even without an air bag (absent from most pickups, unfortunately), the Sonoma/S-Series trucks move to the top of the list of small pickups, foreign and domestic, based on their overall quality, engineering and presentation. Good work, GM. But, ahm, how 'bout getting a bag in these trucks — soon?

Ride, acceleration, handling: In the two-wheel-drive Sonoma/S-Series equipped with the 2.2-liter inline four and five-speed manual, a triumvirate of excellence.

Ride is car-like. Handling has been improved by the use of a stiffer, box-type frame that — in conjunction with other suspension fixes — reduces body shake and shimmy.

Acceleration is surprisingly good. That little four-cylinder engine is gutsy as hell.

Mileage: In the cited test vehicles, about 23 to the gallon (20-gallon tank, estimated 450-mile range on usable volume of regular unleaded), running driver only with absolutely no cargo under the equivalent of test-track conditions.

Price note: GM swears that these new trucks will be as affordable as the models they're replacing, after accounting for equipment changes. Hee, hee. The Chevrolet S-Series pickups (then called the S-10) closed the 1993-model year with retail prices ranging from $9,655 to $16,310. Dealer invoices were $8,738 to $14,761.

The GMC Sonoma trucks closed the year with retail prices ranging from $9,806 to $16,613. Dealer invoices were $8,874 to $15,035.

New-model prices most certainly will be higher. Understandable, given the changes in the vehicles. But, for the life of me, I see no reason to pay one cent more for a GMC Sonoma than I'd pay for Chevrolet S-Series pick-up.

Hometowns: The Sonoma/S-Series pickups are assembled in Moraine, Ohio; Pontiac, Mich., and Shreveport, La.

7

The Brady Bunch

Minivans For The Whole Family

CHEVROLET Astro Minivan

With Notes on the GMC Truck Safari

The Chevrolet Astro is a motorized bulldog, a mutt of a minivan that's found a home in the heart of Middle America. More than half of all Astros are sold in the central and southern states, where they've developed a cult following among middle and working-class families.

That the Astro has a following at all is odd. The Astro and its identical twin, the GMC Truck Safari, came as hurried responses to Chrysler Corp.'s minivans, which arrived in 1984.

The Astro/Safari minivans came in 1985. But at their debut, they seemed dressed for the wrong party.

Chrysler's minivans, for example, showed up with front-wheel drive and car-like handling and design. The Astro/Safari minivans came as rear-wheel drive models with truck-like styling and performance. That's because GM originally planned to sell at least 60 percent of its Astro/Safari models to commercial customers, to be used as delivery and service trucks.

But something happened on the way to market. Buck-stretching families in search of all-in-one transportation discovered the Astro/Safari, and mostly liked what they saw for the money.

Complaints: engine housing intrudes into passenger compartment

Praise: Top marks for safety and utility

Head-turning Quotient: Woof!

Ride, Acceleration, Handling: Decent, but this is a truck — not a car

Brakes: Good

Suggested Retail Price: $15,605 - $18,265

Mileage: About 18 MPG

U.S. Content: 90%

Chevrolet Astro Minivan

The Astro/Safari could seat eight people and carry all of their overnight bags. The minivans could be turned into cargo vans by removing the middle and rear seats. Their sublime truckiness actually enhanced their appeal in rural communities, particularly in southern states, where rear-wheel-drive vehicles can run winter-long with little fear of snow.

In the Central states, where snow is a concern, new four-wheel-drive Astro/Safari models were welcomed warmly. That was in 1990, the same year GM introduced its super-sleek APV minivans.

Industry pundits predicted that the APV's would eclipse the Astro/Safari models.

They were wrong.

Background 1994: Both the Astro and the Safari get standard facial air bags in the new model year, and both get front- and side-door guard beams to reduce the risk of injury in side-impact crashes. Stronger B pillars, the central pillars, have been put in place to increase roll-over roof-crush protection. And like many cars and trucks for 1994, the Astro and Safari are dumping ozone-harmful chloroflourocarbon (CFC-R12) air-conditioner refrigerants in favor of the ozone-friendly R-134a type.

Improved 4.3-liter V-6 engines, a slightly reworked instrument panel, and improved rust-protection also mark changes in the 1994 Astro and Safari minivans, both of which are available in extended (186.8-inches long overall) and standard bodies (176.8 inches).

The standard engine for all two-wheel-rear-drive Astro and Safari models is an electronically fuel-injected 4.3-liter V-6 rated 165 horsepower at 4,000 rpm with a maximum torque of 235 foot-pounds at 2,000 rpm. Four-wheel-drive models get a standard 4.3-liter V-6 rated 200 horsepower at 4,400 rpm with a maximum torque of 260 foot-pounds at 3,600 rpm.

Each of the V-6 engines is equipped with a counter-rotating balance shaft, which turns in the opposite direction of the crankshaft, thus canceling harmonic vibrations and providing quieter, smoother engine performance.

An electronically controlled four-speed automatic transmission is standard in all Astro and Safari minivans.

Standard brakes include power front discs/rear drums with a four-wheel, anti-lock brake system.

The Astro and Safari each have three different trim categories: the base CS, upgraded CL, and "luxury touring" LT for the Astro; and the base SLX, upgraded SLE, and luxury SLT for the Safari.

Towing/payload capacities: The Astro and Safari minivans can carry up to eight people. They can handle cargo weighing from 1,697 to 1,914 lbs., depending on minivan size and equipment. The minivans can be outfitted to pull trailer weights up to 5,500 lbs.

Complaints: True to their cargo-van heritage, the Astro and Safari are afflicted by their front-engine housing which invades the passenger compartment, creating an obstructive hump. That hump restricts leg-room for normal-size, adult front-seat passengers.

Praise: Safety improvements in the new Astro/Safari minivans get top marks. Overall construction is excellent. Top marks for utility.

Head-turning quotients:

- Astro — Woof!
- Safari — Woof! Woof!

Ride, acceleration and handling: The Astro and Safari ride and feel like the trucks they are. They are *not* uncomfortable. But they are bouncy, especially on less-than-well-kept roads.

Acceleration in the tested 1994 Astro LT two-wheel-drive, equipped with the 160-horsepower V-6, was sure and even. No jack-rabbit, 0-to-60 stuff; just a nice, good pull to higher revs. Braking was good in the tested minivan.

Mileage: In the standard-body Astro LT, about 18 to the gallon (27-gallon tank, estimated 474-mile range on usable volume of regular unlead-

Top marks for

utility.

ed), running mostly highway with one to three occupants.

Sound system: In the standard-body Astro LT, optional six-speaker AM/FM stereo radio and cassette with graphic equalizer, by GM/Delco. Good boogie.

Price note: The Chevrolet Astro passenger minivans closed the 1993-model year with retail prices ranging from $15,605 to $18,265, and dealer's invoice prices ranging from $14,123 to $16,530. Comparable GMC Safari mini's closed at retail prices ranging from $15,824 to $18,484, with dealer's prices ranging from $14,321 to $16,728.

There is absolutely no logical reason to pay more for a Safari than an Astro — no reason at all.

Expect a five-percent or so jump in 1994 Astro/Safari prices to help cover the cost of added safety equipment and engine improvements. Still, you will be able to deal on these models, which offer a lot per buck paid.

Hometown: The Chevrolet Astro and GMC Safari are made on the same assembly lines by the same workers the same way using the same tools and components at the same plant in Baltimore, Md.

Complaints: V6 engine should be standard

Praise: The best minivans available

Head-turning Quotient: Middle-class classics

Ride, Acceleration, Handling: Good to excellent

Brakes: Very good

Suggested Retail Price: $14,248 - $24,059

Mileage: About 21 MPG

U.S. Content: 75%

DODGE Caravan

With Notes on the Plymouth Voyager and Chrysler Town & Country

This is in praise of Caesar, former Chrysler Chairman Lee A. Iacocca, a gruff, mercurial sort who knew how to run a car company.

Proof of that is the the Dodge Caravan and its identical twin, the Plymouth Voyager — and their rich cousin, the Chrysler Town & Country.

Chrysler Corp. opened the minivan market in 1984. Ten years later, with new and improved models, it still owns it.

That is some kind of feat, considering the number of car companies, foreign and domestic, that have been trying to take Chrysler's minivan crown. Judging from the looks and performance of the 1994 Dodge Caravan, they'll just have to try harder.

The new Dodge Caravan comes with dual-front air bags, a new 3.8-liter V-6 engine, an improved 3.3-liter V-6, side-door beams to increase side-impact crash protection, remote keyless entry system, a redesigned instrument panel, and a freshened exterior appearance — among numerous other improvements.

And the thing of it is that the Caravan/Voyager/Town & Country already ranked as the best minivans available.

Dodge Caravan

Ol' Lee used to call the minivan "Chrysler's Franchise." Indeed, that's been the case. Back in the late 1980s, when things were once again going to hell at the nation's third largest auto company, minivans saved Chrysler from perdition. Iacocca, who presided over the original minivan launch, vowed never to abandon the product through neglect.

"We're going to keep improving it," he said before retiring last year.

Look at the 1994 Dodge Caravan. The man kept his word.

Background: How do you make best better? You look for shortcomings in what you've got. You go to your buyers, ask them what they want, what they're willing to pay for. Then, you give them more than they expected for their money. Chrysler repeatedly has used that formula to keep its minivans ahead of the pack. Here we go again in the 1994-model year.

The use of dual-side air bags, including passenger-side knee bolsters, should increase the already high consumer confidence in the safety of the Caravan/Voyager/Town & Country. Ditto the new front and side-door beams and the new, four-wheel anti-lock brake system.

The anti-lock system is optional on the company's two-wheel-front-drive minivans; but it's sold as standard equipment on the all-wheel-drive models.

Also optional are the built-in child safety seats, which will be sold in 1994 with a reclining back feature.

New standard equipment includes the extensively reworked instrument panel, which is tilted upward in the Caravan/Voyager/Town & Country for better visibility. The "center" console has been moved left for easier driver access, and has been outfitted with an open lower bin (a hinged bin on the T & C) for storage of compact discs and things. New cupholders adjacent to the panel are deeper and wider, capable of holding small and large cups. Left unchanged is the panel's "message center," which reports on various vehicle conditions — still located in a slit above the instrument panel.

Ah, the engines! Buyers of the Town & Country and the Grand Caravan/Voyager, the extended models, asked Chrysler for a more powerful V-6. They get it in 1994 with an optional, fuel-injected 3.8-liter V-6 rated 162 horsepower at 4,400 rpm. Maximum torque is 213 foot-pounds at 3,600 rpm. That's 12 more horsepower and 10 foot-pounds more torque, or twisting power, than was available in the 3.3-liter V-6 used in the top-line minivans in 1993.

A revised 3.3-liter V-6 also provides 162 horsepower, but works harder and runs less smoothly than the 3.8-liter V-6 to reach that goal. Top horsepower in the new 3.3-liter V-6 comes in at 4,800 rpm. A max torque of 194 foot-pounds shows up at 3,600 rpm.

A 135-horsepower, inline four-cylinder engine is standard in the regular Caravan/Voyager. A 142-horsepower, 3-liter V-6 is standard in the extended versions of those minivans.

A five-speed manual transmission is standard on Chrysler's regular-size, base minivans. A three-speed automatic comes standard on the extended (Grand) minivans. A four-speed automatic is standard on the Town & Country. Of course, buyers can get automatic transmissions as optional equipment,

Standard brakes include power, vented front discs/rear drums.

Complaints: The four-cylinder engine should be dropped from Chrysler Corp.'s minivan lineup. Chrysler says it retains the thing because it's fuel efficient. I say that it's underpowered, especially if seven people are sitting in the minivan. The 142-horsepower, 3-liter V-6 should be made standard. After all, we're not talking economy cars here.

Praise: As a group, the Dodge Caravan, Plymouth Voyager, and Chrysler Town & Country simply are the best minivans available. I've driven all three models. I've driven a version of the Caravan/Voyager every year since 1984; and I've driven the competition. Some minivans have come close to matching Chrysler's models. But no one has caught up with 'em, yet.

Head-turning quotients:
• Caravan/Voyager, standard and extended — high and pleasant, middle-class classics.
• Town & Country — drips wealth.

If you show up at a PTA meeting in this one, bring your checkbook. You obviously can afford to make a contribution.

Ride, acceleration and handling: All three models offer excellent ride and handling. They feel like big sedans.

Acceleration is very good-to-excellent with the 3-liter and 3.8-liter V-6 engines. The 2.5-liter inline four is a wimpmeister in Chrysler's minivan lineup. I don't know what the hell it's doing there.

Braking is very good in all three minivans. Go for the anti-lock option where applicable.

Mileage: In the front-wheel-drive Grand Caravan with the standard 3-liter V-6, about 21 to the gallon (20-gallon tank, estimated 420-mile range on usable volume of regular unleaded), running with four occupants and light cargo.

Sound system: In the tested Grand Caravan — four-speaker AM/FM stereo radio and cassette with Dolby sound. Very good.

Price note: Dodge Caravan passenger vans closed the 1993-model year with retail prices ranging from $14,248 to $24,059. Dealer prices on those models went from $13,023 to $21,682. Chrysler Town & Country retail prices ranged from $25,713 to $27,704, with dealer's prices on those models ranging from $23,307 to $25,060.

Expect some significant price hikes to help cover the cost of changes and new equipment in the 1994 models. But, take heart. Chrysler has no intention of bleeding its minivan franchise by gouging its customers. The new, suggested retail prices will be just that — suggestions. You can suggest a lower price in bargaining.

Hometowns: The regular Caravan/Voyager models are assembled in Windsor, Ontario, Canada. The extended versions of those models, as well as their companion luxury cruiser, the Chrysler Town & Country, are assembled in St. Louis, Mo.

FORD Aerostar

With Notes on the Windstar Minivan

Complaints: Wind and engine noise

Praise: Overall excellent construction

Head-turning Quotient: Dated, stale, boring

Ride, Acceleration, Handling: Decent. Truck-like

Brakes: Very good

Suggested Retail Price: $14,321 - $17,868

Mileage: About 18 MPG

U.S. Content: 90%

The Swedes came in the Summer of '88. There were 60 of them, young musicians of the Eskilstuna Gardet. Their families hosted our kids, the Arlington Youth Wind Ensemble, in their homes and country the summer before. We were returning the favor.

Vans and wagons were needed to ferry the visitors to and fro during their two-week stay in Northern Virginia. I was elected minister of transportation, and asked to find several vehicles.

I came up with three 1988 models — the Ford Aerostar XLT minivan/wagon, the Chevrolet Caprice station wagon and, just in case our guests got homesick, a Volvo 240 station wagon.

The Swedish kids barely paid attention to the Volvo; and they noted the then-linear Caprice wagon with transient curiosity. But we couldn't keep them out of the Aerostar.

"So biiiig. Such a pretty limo," said one of the students who stayed in our home. "We have wagons in Sweden, but nothing like this. This is exciting!" she said of the Aerostar.

And so it went for the entire two weeks, with the Aerostar serving as commuter bus, a cargo van for dozens of instruments and, in one case, an ambulance. One of the Swedish kids broke his leg during a soccer game. A doctor among us performed first aid. We removed middle seats from the Aerostar, placed a long, thick foam cushion on the floor, hoisted the kid aboard and carried him to the hospital.

It was some kind of summer, some kind of minivan. Of course, we have photos, one of which is prominently displayed atop a piano in our living room. Our daughter, Binta, is in the picture with two of our Swedish house guests, Helene and Angnetta. They're standing in front of the Aerostar.

Background: The Aerostar, introduced in May 1985 as a 1986 model, is on its way out. It's been a good minivan, but no competition for the Chrysler models. It will be replaced, probably in the 1995-model year, by a more-Chrysler-than-thou vehicle, the Windstar.

Accordingly, there aren't many changes in the 1994 Aerostar, other than a new, rear high-mounted stop lamp. The "new" Aerostar essentially is the same as it was in 1992, when a driver's air bag and knee bolster were added as standard equipment, and when Ford made some modest exterior and interior changes to the vehicle.

Aerostar models are available in regular (174.9 inches long overall) and extended (190.3 inches) bodies. Both bodies are available with two-wheel-rear drive or four-wheel drive.

The Aerostar runs with a standard, electronically fuel-injected 3-liter V-6 engine rated 135 horsepower at 4,600 rpm. Maximum torque is 160 foot-pounds at 2,800 rpm. That engine can come with either a five-speed manual, or an electronically controlled, four-speed automatic transmission.

An optional, electronically fuel-injected 4-liter V-6 is available. It has a horsepower rating of 155 at 4,000 rpm. Maximum torque is 230 foot-pounds at 2,400 rpm. A heavy-duty four-speed automatic transmission is available with the 4-liter V-6.

Standard brakes include power front discs/rear drums with a rear anti-lock system.

Aerostar trim packages include the Standard Van, XL wagon, XL Plus wagon, the luxury XLT, and the super-luxury Eddie Bauer Wagon.

Towing/passenger/payload capacities: The Aerostar can carry from five to seven passengers and can handle cargo payloads ranging from 1,600 lbs. to 1,950 lbs. The minivan can be equipped to pull trailer weights up to 5,500 lbs.

Complaints: Some Aerostar owners have complained about stalling in the 3-liter V-6; but there appears to be no consistent defect pattern.

In the last-tested 1993 Aerostar XLT — two-wheel drive, regular body

Ford Aerostar

— wind and engine noise were high, especially at highway speeds. The driver's seat was adequate, but not as comfortable as it should have been in a luxury minivan.

Praise: Overall excellent construction and presentation. I've driven an Aerostar sample almost every year since the introduction of the vehicle. With the exception of the last two years, each new model was in some way better than the predecessor.

Head-turning quotient: Dated, stale, boring.

Ride, acceleration and handling: In the 1993 Aerostar XLT, ride and handling were truck-like, more truck-like, in fact, than the ride and handling of the comparable Chevrolet Astro/GMC Safari minivans. Acceleration with the optional 4-liter V-6 was excellent. Braking was very good.

Mileage: In the 1993 Aerostar XLT — about 18 miles per gallon (21-gallon tank, estimated 379-mile range on usable volume of regular unleaded), running mostly highway with one to four occupants and light cargo.

Sound system: Four-speaker AM/FM stereo radio and cassette with graphic equalizer, installed by Ford. Very good.

Price: Aerostar retail prices ranged from $14,321 to $17,868 at the end of the 1993-model year. Dealer prices on those models went from $12,728 to $15,849. Probably no price increases in 1994. In fact, the 1994-model year might be the best time to buy the Aerostar, inasmuch as it's about to cede the stage to Windstar. Most certainly, you can go for discounts on this one.

Windstar notes: The Windstar will be based on the Ford Taurus drivetrain, which means that it will be front-wheel-drive in standard form. Dual air bags and a four-speed automatic transmission will be standard. Plans are to bring out a Windstar body that offers more usable space than the Chrysler minivans.

Hometown: The Ford Aerostar is assembled in St. Louis, Mo.

MERCURY Villager

With Notes on the Nissan Quest

Nina Fiore knows lots about music and graphic arts; but Nina don't know nothin' 'bout minivans.

Leo "The Caller" knows lots about sports cars and sedans; but Leo don't know nothin' 'bout minivans, either.

Nina and Leo are two of my friends and critics. Nina, I know well. Leo,

Mercury Villager

I've never met in person. He just phones me all the time. Both of 'em have opinions on everything.

Take Nina. She took one look at the new Mercury Villager LS minivan and got nasty.

"Whattaya doin'? Some kind of family-values column? Like we need another kind of minivan on the road? Aaargghhhh! I hate minivans and everything they stand for," she said.

Leo's something else. To my knowledge, he's never seen a Villager up close. But when I told him on the phone that I was reviewing an all-new minivan, he was underwhelmed. "Gee, well, maybe next week you can do something interesting," he said.

Turkeys! They think minivans are jive because they're driven by lots of suburban moms and pops. They figure that anything built to carry seven people can't possibly be fun. They haven't driven the Villager.

"And never will," said Nina.

You can't please everybody.

Background: The Mercury Villager/Nissan Quest were introduced in 1992 as 1993 models. They are mechanically and structurally identical minivans. Their differences are purely cosmetic. The Villager, with its well-decorated rear end and light-bar front grille, wins the beauty contest. The Quest has all of the appeal of a small cargo van.

Ironically, Nissan did most of the engineering and design work on the

Praise: Seating and cargo flexibility

Head-turning Quotient: Thumbs up

Ride, Acceleration, Handling: Double aces, except poor acceleration at higher altitudes

Brakes: Top marks

Suggested Retail Price: $16,515 - $22,090

Mileage: About 20 MPG

U.S. Content: 70%

You can change

the seats around

14 different ways.

minivans. Ford does all of the assembly.

Because of their intro as 1993 models, little change was expected for the 1994 Villager/Quest minivans. But there are some notable improvements, including a standard driver's air bag, improved radiator, ozone-friendly air conditioner refrigerant, and an electrical-system change designed to prolong battery life.

Both the Villager and Quest are equipped with a 3-liter, electronically fuel-injected V-6 rated 151 horsepower at 4,800 rpm, with a maximum torque of 174 foot-pounds at 4,400 rpm. A four-speed automatic overdrive transmission, with an overdrive lockout switch, is standard.

Use of the overdrive lockout increases engine torque, which is desirable under certain circumstances, such as moving uphill with a load. But more torque means more work. More work requires more energy, which increases fuel consumption.

Standard brakes include power front discs/rear drums with a four-wheel, anti-lock system.

The Mercury Villager has three trim levels — GS Van, base GS passenger, and luxury LS passenger. The Nissan Quest is available as a cargo van, and as base XE and luxury GXE passenger minivans.

Both are front-engine, front-wheel-drive vehicles.

Towing, payload, seating capacities: Both the Villager and Quest can be equipped to pull a 3,500-lbs. trailer. Maximum onboard payload capacity, including passengers in this case, is 1,290 lbs. Depending on seating arrangement, the Villager and Quest can carry from five to seven people.

Complaint: My outstanding complaint, the absence of an air bag in the 1993 models, has been taken care of in the 1994 Villager/Quest minivans.

Praise: There are many things to love in both vehicles. Take seating and cargo flexibility. You can change the seats around 14 different ways to accommodate bodies and stuff in the Villager/Quest minivans. That's more flexibility than is available in any other minivan at the moment; and it's accomplished through the use of track seating.

Let's say you get a Villager that seats seven. You can carry seven people. Or, you can take out the middle seat and slide the rear seat all the way up to the front seat to get 126-cubic feet of cargo capacity. Or, you can turn the middle of the van into a dining room by removing some seats and using the folded backs of others as tables.

Head-turning quotients:

• Thumbs up for the Villager.

• Thumbs wiggle-waggle for the Quest, which has a decidedly unattractive grille treatment.

Ride, acceleration and handling: Double aces for ride and handling, competitive with the Chrysler and Toyota minivans. Handling around curves is impressive for both the Villager and the Quest.

Acceleration gets negative marks at high altitudes. Lots and lots of unintended downshifting in both minivans under those conditions. Flat-lands acceleration is excellent. Braking gets top marks, too.

Mileage: About 20 miles per gallon (20-gallon tank, estimated 390-mile range on usable volume of regular unleaded), running mostly high-way with one-to-five occupants and about 500 lbs. of cargo.

Price note: The Mercury Villager closed the 1993-model year with retail prices ranging from $16,515 to $22,090. Dealer invoice prices were from $14,698 to $19,605. Nissan Quest retail prices ranged from $17,195 to $21,800, with a dealer invoice spread of $14,908 to $18,901.

Equipment changes and growing demand mean higher 1994 prices. But keep in mind that there is no logical, functional, qualitative reason to pay more for a Villager than you would for a Quest. Comparison shop.

Hometown: The Mercury Villager and Nissan Quest are assembled by Ford Motor Co. in Avon Lake, Ohio.

PONTIAC Trans Sport

With Notes on the Chevrolet Lumina and Oldsmobile Silhouette

The thrill is gone.
The Pontiac Trans Sport and its identical siblings, the Lumina and Silhouette APV minivans once excited me.
No longer.
The thrill is gone.
I used to like their wild, rakish, long, wide, sheer-drop windshields. Used to love their oh-my-gosh behinds with the two sets of corner-mounted backlights descending from top to middle, looking like some cascade of red, red, red.
I used to say, "Oh, wow!," seeing those lights move through the night.
But,
Hey,
The thrill is gone.
And even with the 1994 fixes —
The industry's first power-sliding door,
The freshened front ends with their big-eyed, bug-eyed headlamps,
The standard driver's air bag and

Praise: A terrific value for the dollar

Ride, Acceleration, Handling: Decent — as long as you get the 3.8L V-6

Brakes: Decent

Suggested Retail Price: $14,600 - $15,800

Mileage: About 17 MPG

U.S. Content: 90%

Pontiac Trans Sport

The new,
Rear,
Center
High-mounted stoplights
(CHMSLs)
(What the hell for?) —
The thrill ain't coming back.
Found so many new minivans to love, you see?
Hell, I've even gone out with the Chevrolet Astro and GMC Safari and
had a good time.
Real good time.
Fantastic, even.
But I just can't hang with the Trans Sport/Lumina/Silhouette no mo'.
Don't like their long, redesigned, but still too long dashboards.
Don't like their general heaviness.
Don't like the stuffed feel of their interiors.
And I sho' don't like
The way they look no mo' — see?
Like they look like some date in a Star Trek suit

*With Star Trek medallions
And belt-buckles and stuff,
Showin' up at a formal State Department dinner
Where everybody's
Wearin' gowns
And tuxedos.
I'm just not into that no mo'.
It ain't cool, ain't hip, ain't flip.
It's a crazy trip.
And if you show up at my door lookin' like that
Minivan or not,
I'm goin' without ya.*

Background: GM introduced the Trans Sport, Lumina, Silhouette in 1990, in large measure because the company thought it missed the mark with its earlier Astro/Safari minivans, which now have a strong following.

By comparison, the APV triumvirate, GM's front-wheel-drive minivans, never did all that well. The biggest seller, the Chevrolet Lumina, had 63,141 sales in its introduction year and a skimpy 43,781 in 1992. The best-looking of the bunch, the Trans Sport sold a measly 30,247 in 1992. The Silhouette! Have mercy! Forget it — an anemic 15,982 sales in 1982.

You get the feelin' that the market is trying to tell General Motors something about these models? I do. GM does, too; and it's workin' on replacements as you're reading this.

In a way, it's all too bad, because the GM APVs are pretty good when you get beneath the fru-fru. Their dent-resistant composite plastic bodies are great. They're loaded with power, convenience options — the latest example of which is that push-button sliding side door. They can seat up to seven people and be outfitted to tow up to 3,000 lbs.

The base engine in the GM APVs is a 3.1-liter V-6 rated 120 horsepower at 4,400 rpm. Maximum torque is 175 foot-pounds at 2,200 rpm. The standard transmission with that engine is a three-speed automatic which, altogether, amounts to an unimpressive powertrain package.

You would be far better off with the optional 3.8-liter V-6, rated 170 horsepower at 4,800 rpm, with a maximum torque of 225 foot-pounds at 3,200 rpm. The standard transmission with this engine is a very nice four-speed automatic.

Standard brakes include power front discs/rear drums with a four-wheel, anti-lock system.

Complaints: You heard 'em.

Praise: You heard that, too. Except, add kudos for the optional traction-control system.

I used to like their

wild, rakish, long,

wide, sheer-drop

windshields, but

the thrill is gone.

Head-turning quotients:
- Trans Sport, the good.
- Lumina, the bad.
- Silhouette, the ugly.

Ride, acceleration and handling: Forget the 3.1 liter V-6/three-speed automatic combinations. Grunters supreme. You're better off with the 3.8-liter V-6 models, which offer excellent acceleration and very decent ride, handling and braking.

Mileage: In the 3.8-liter APV's, about 17 to the gallon (estimated 330-mile range on usable volume of regular unleaded), under a variety of driving and load conditions.

Sound system: A variety of available GM/Delco systems, mostly excellent. My favorite is the Delco AM/FM stereo radio and cassette with five-band graphic equalizer. Excellent.

Price note: At the end of the 1993-model year: Chevrolet Lumina APV retail prices ranged from $14,600 to $15,800 with a dealer invoice spread of $12,854 to $13,825. The luxury Oldsmobile Silhouette was priced at $19,499 with a dealer's invoice of $17,646. The Pontiac Trans Sport was priced at $16,689 with a dealer invoice of $15,104.

Even with equipment changes, I expect GM to look toward value pricing on its APV's for 1994. I mean, let's face it. Nobody's rushing to buy 'em.

Hometown: The Trans Sport, Lumina and Silhouette APVs are assembled in Tarrytown, N.Y.

8

The Rough Riders

Four-Wheel Drive Sport Utility Vehicles

FORD Explorer

Complaints: Bouncy	
Praise: Good-looking utility	
Head-turning Quotient: High and friendly	
Ride, Acceleration, Handling: A competent runner	
Brakes: Good	
Suggested Retail Price: $21,000 - $26,000	
Mileage: About 19 MPG	
U.S. Content: 85%	

Some vehicles look at you and say, "Yo, man! Fun time. Let's run!" Others look at you and say, "Hey, dude. Better put on some old jeans. We got work to do." It's important to know what's being said before you sign the sales agreement. Otherwise, you could wind up buying weekends of toil and sweat instead of fun in the sun.

Trouble is, some vehicles speak out of both sides of their grilles. For example, there is the Eddie Bauer edition of the four-door, four-wheel drive Ford Explorer that I test-drove. It's really pretty, with its metallic twilight blue body and its light sandalwood-colored skirts.

It has wraparound front bumpers, flush-mounted glass, limousine-style doors, beautiful aluminum wheels. Inside, it's all plushed out with velour seats and power everything — locks, windows and remote-control mirrors. All of that prettiness seems to smile at you, to beckon you to hop in and crank the Explorer's big V-6 and head for the hills.

Hah! It's a setup, a trick. If you want to know what the Explorer's really saying, you'd better lower its rear seats and check out all that cargo space — 81.6 cubic feet of it, more room than anything in its class.

So watcha think you're gonna be doing with all that space, huh? Car-

Ford Explorer

rying beach balls and picnic baskets? Get real. That shed has to be cleaned out, and all of the junk hauled away. Yeah, and on your trip back home, stop by the hardware store and pick up that lumber that came in two weeks ago and . . . have a nice weekend.

Background: The Explorer was introduced in mid-1990 as a 1991 model, replacing the Ford Bronco II, Ford's former mid-size sport-utility vehicle that came with two doors only. The Explorer comes in two-and four-door versions, both of which are available in the least-expensive XL model and the top-line Eddie Bauer edition.

The mid-priced version is marketed as the Explorer XLT. The XLT offers better value for the dollar, especially if you have a family of four or more people and can live without the fancy extras.

For 1994, Ford is going whole-hog with an even more luxurious Explorer, the Explorer Limited.

Complaints: The Explorer is quite bouncy, too bouncy for some tastes — which is weird. The thing handles better than most sports-utility vehicles on curves and it has a very car-like ride on decent roads. But on less that perfectly smooth streets, whoa! It bounces like a hyperactive basketball. Ford has improved the suspension and so for 1994 it should handle better on rough roads.

Praise: High marks for utility, and for exterior and interior design. Unless you're willing to pay twice as much for a Range Rover, you won't find a better-looking workhorse anywhere. After loading up the cargo bay, you can hitch 5,600 lbs. to the Explorer's rear bumper. This beauty's a beast when it comes to hauling stuff.

Head-turning quotient: High and friendly. People really liked this one.

Acceleration and braking: The Explorer is equipped with a four-liter, fuel injected V-6 rated a 160 horsepower. It's a competent runner on the highway.

The brakes are power front discs and rear drums with a four-wheel anti-lock system. It stops quickly.

Sound system: AM / FM stereo radio and cassette, Ford JBL system. Excellent.

Mileage: About 19 to the gallon (19.3-gallon tank, estimated 345 mile range).

Price: The Eddie Bauer edition lists for about $24,300, the XLT $24,000 and the XL $21,000. The Explorer Limited carries a hefty $27,500 sticker.

Purse strings note: It's a buy (one of the best-selling vehicles in America) but it's a better buy in the XLT or XL versions. You don't need all of that fancy Eddie Bauer stuff. You'll spend more time working than partying with this one.

Hometown: The Ford Explorer is made in Louisville, Ky.

GMC Truck Jimmy Sport-Utility Vehicle

With Notes on the Chevrolet S-Blazer

It was a white truck with four doors and a not-quite-gray interior. It smelled new, and I liked that. Some folks get excited over cologne. I get goose bumps over "new-car smell," even when I find it in a truck like the GMC Truck Jimmy SLE.

There is a ritual to settling into a new vehicle, certain semi-sacred procedures to follow. Some people hop in and start touching and squeezing everything. They play with all of the buttons before keying the ignition and zipping off.

Me, I'm slow. I walk around the vehicle, try to get a feel for its dimensions. And if it's a particularly attractive set of wheels, I sort of stand back and watch it. Afterwards, I always open the door gently, run my hands over the steering wheel, and just sit there for a while — and sniff.

Complaints: Flirting with boredom

Praise: Solidly built. Very smooth engine

Head-turning Quotient: Tepid suburban embrace

Ride, Acceleration, Handling: Excellent

Brakes: Needed squeezing

Suggested Retail Price: $15,639 - $19,298

Mileage: About 17 MPG

U.S. Content: 90%

GMC Truck Jimmy

Ahhh, the fragrance of fresh vinyl, new leather and high-quality cloth, accented by a hint of gasoline and oil! The test Jimmy had all of that, minus the leather. The seats were of cloth, but it was good-feeling, quality material.

Anyway, the Jimmy kept its wonderful aroma for several days — until my spouse suggested that I truck some breakfast to one of our youngsters, who had bypassed that meal in pursuit of an organized activity she thought more important. Of course, the breakfast plate made it to the floor of the Jimmy before it ever got to our daughter. Thus, there was this mess of bacon, eggs, pancakes and maple syrup, which seemed to take all day to clean up. But in the end, the cleansing was for naught. The Jimmy's smell was gone.

Background: The GMC Truck Jimmy is exactly the same vehicle as the Chevrolet S-Blazer — the small version of the full-size Chevrolet Blazer, which is the same thing as the full-size GMC Truck Yukon. What can I say? GM has a fetish for matched pairs.

Anyway, both the Jimmy and S-Blazer are compact sport-utility vehicles, suvvies, meaning that they are covered trucks deigned to carry passengers and cargo. For 1994, these compact suvvies get a number of "refinements" — the auto industry's term for minor improvements.

Changes include side-door beams to improve crash protection in side-impact accidents, improved anti-corrosion treatment, tweaked V-6 engines, a new 60/40 split front bench seat, and a new high-mounted stop lamp in the rear of the vehicle.

But bigtime changes are in store for the Jimmy and S-Blazer in the 1995-model year, when General Motors Corp. redesigns those vehicles, giving them a miniature Chevrolet Suburban appearance. The 1995 models essentially will be the same size as the current editions. But they will be sleeker, rounder, and probably will come with at least a driver's air bag.

Like the current Jimmy and S-Blazer, the 1995 models will feature four-wheel, anti-lock braking systems as standard equipment.

Both the 1994 Jimmy and S-Blazer are available with two or four doors; and both are offered in two-wheel-rear drive and four-wheel drive.

Two versions of General Motors Corp.'s 4.3-liter V-6 engine are available for the Jimmy/S-Blazer. One has a horsepower rating of 165 at 4,000 rpm with a maximum torque of 235 at 2,400 rpm. The other 4.3-liter V-6 is rated 200 horsepower at 4,500 rpm with a maximum torque of 260 horsepower at 3,600 rpm.

The 160-horsepower V-6 is standard with a five-speed manual transmission. The 200-horsepower V-6 is standard with a four-speed automatic.

Standard Jimmy/S-Blazer brakes include power front discs/rear drums with a four-wheel, anti-lock system. Both vehicles have three trim levels. For the Blazer, there are the base Standard, mid-line Tahoe, and top-line Tahoe LT. The Jimmy lineup includes the base SLS, mid-line SLE and top-line SLT.

Towing, payload and seating capacities: The Jimmy and S-Blazer can seat four people comfortably, five with a squeeze. Both suvvies can be equipped to carry cargo weighing up to 1,453 pounds. Both can be outfitted to pull trailers weighing up to 5,750 pounds.

Complaints: The new exterior/interior designs can't come soon enough. The current Jimmy and S-Blazer aren't ugly; but they are flirting with boredom.

Also, GMC Truck and Chevrolet need to pay fanatical attention to fit and finish. In the four-door, 1993 Jimmy SLE 4x4, the floor-mounted center console was loose and wiggly. In a two-door, 1994 S-Blazer Tahoe LT, some plastic molding bordering the headliner was out of sync. Small stuff — but not the kind of stuff you want in otherwise excellent vehicles.

Praise: Overall excellent construction — the 1994 Jimmy SLE is a solidly built truck. Ditto its tested, companion S-Blazer Tahoe. High praise for the 200-horsepower V-6. It's one of the smoothest engines around. Splendid truck acceleration.

Head-turning quotient: Tepid suburban embrace. Perhaps, if people could have sniffed the Jimmy SLE's interior before it was splattered with pancakes, their attraction would've turned to passion.

Ride, handling and braking: In the 1994 Jimmy SLE 4x4 with the

One of the smoothest engines around.

200 horsepower V-6, excellent ride and handling.

Back-seat passengers usually complain in trucks. But the Jimmy's rear riders were mostly pleased.

Brakes in the 1993 Jimmy SLE and the '94 S-Blazer Tahoe left something to be desired. I had to squeeze 'em to please 'em. Maybe it was a truck thing; I dunno. I just kept squeezin'; they seemed to respond best to that.

High praise for the 200-horsepower V-6. It's one of the smoothest engines around.

Mileage: In the tested Jimmy SLE 4x4 with the 200-horsepower V-6, about 17 to the gallon (20-gallon tank, estimated 330-mile range on usable volume of regular unleaded), carrying one to four occupants and light cargo.

Sound system: Four-speaker AM/FM stereo radio and cassette with compact disc installed by GM/Delco. Good jazz, rap, and better soul. Boogied so much, almost lost control. No more jammin' behind the wheel. Next time I listen, I'm gonna park this deal.

Price note: GMC Jimmy prices for 1994 range from $15,639 to $19,298. Dealer's invoice prices go from $14,253 to $17,465. By comparison, closing 1993 GMC Jimmy prices ranged from $15,022 to $18,287, with dealer's invoice prices spanning $13,595 to $16,550, according to figures from Automobile Invoice Service in San Jose, Calif. Expect 1994 S-Blazer prices to experience similar increases. Also, compare S-Blazer and Jimmy prices very carefully. They are the same vehicles with different nameplates.

Hometowns: The GMC Truck Jimmy and Chevrolet S-Blazer are assembled in Moraine, Ohio and Pontiac, Mich.

GMC Truck Yukon

With a note on the Chevrolet Blazer

It was day of obligation, which meant a day of hauling. I could've used a nice minivan, or employed a beast. I chose the beast, the full-size, two-door, four-wheel-drive GMC Truck Yukon.

There's a certain approach to such vehicles, even when they wear pretty paint. The first rule is respect, and this is how you go about it — before climbing into the truck, you walk around it to get an idea of its dimensions. This is important if your hauling routes involve urban traffic. The Yukon is big, very big. That means you don't have much road room for error. No swerving in and out of lanes. No U-turns.

Next, before reading the Yukon's owner's manual, you should read

GMC Truck Yukon

The Leadership Principles of Attila the Hun. This book will help you understand the responsible uses of fear — that is, how to bully people without getting them angry. To wit: you're in a gargantuan, 4x4 truck. Therefore, you belong in whatever space you occupy. Most people with common sense won't mess with you, especially if you move into that space with some semblance of courtesy.

Finally, read the owner's manual. The Yukon is not a car; nor is it a namby-pamby suburban people hauler, and it does not handle like any of those things. It's a monstrous truck; and if nothing else gets that through your head, the owner's manual certainly will.

Now, then, clean that yard. Lift that bale. Load that truck, and move your tail.

Background: The GMC Yukon is a revised version of the full-size, two-door, 4x4 GMC Jimmy, a sport-utility vehicle that was updated out of existence in 1992. The new model is based on the platform of General Motors Corp.'s C/K pickups — as is the Yukon's identical twin, the full-size Chevrolet Blazer. And that, folks, is all I'm going to say about the Blazer in this section. A full-size Yukon is a full-size Blazer is a full-size Yukon. Period.

The Yukon comes in four-wheel-drive only. A five-speed manual transmission is standard, but recommended only for people who are into body building. For normal folks, GMC's new, optional four-speed automatic

Complaints: Parking in the city is hard	
Praise: A civilian tank	
Head-turning Quotient: People look up to it	
Ride, Acceleration, Handling: It's a *truck*	
Suggested Retail Price: $20,243	
Mileage: About 15 MPG	
U.S. Content: 90%	

transmission — the Hydramatic 4L60-E — is a much more pleasant way to change gears.

New items on the 1994 Yukon include side-door guard beams, an improved 5.7-liter V-8 as the standard engine, an optional 6.5-liter V-8 turbo diesel; also, a rear, center, high-mounted stoplight, new grille, improved anti-corrosion treatment, better parking brakes, and ozone-friendly, air-conditioner refrigerant.

In 1993, the Yukon got a new anti-theft system that is carried over on the 1994 models. Thugs who try to steal the truck by attacking the cylinder-lock sleeve now have to work their way through a hard-steel collar to get to the ignition. They doubtless can do that; but it'll add precious seconds to their ignoble endeavor.

The Yukon's 5.7-liter V-8 engine is rated 210 horsepower at 4,000 rpm, with a maximum torque of 300 foot-pounds at 2,800 rpm. The 6.5-liter V-8 turbo diesel is rated 180 horsepower at 3,400 rpm, with a maximum torque of 360 foot-pounds at 1,700 rpm.

Standard brakes include power front discs/rear drums with a four-wheel, anti-lock system.

The 1994 Yukon is available in two trim categories, the reasonably well-appointed SL and the exceptionally well-appointed SLE.

Towing, cargo, seating capacities: The Yukon can carry five or six people, depending on the chosen seating arrangement. Cargo space is 53 cubic feet with rear seats up and 102.8 cubic feet with rear seats down. It can be equipped to tow up to 7,000 lbs.

Complaints: Parking the Yukon anywhere in the city is hard. And when you get ready to leave a parking spot, you have to be careful not to pull the hood-release lever when attempting to free the parking brake. The levers are too close to each other.

Also, though the Yukon has room to carry lots of stuff, it offers few amenities for rear passengers. Back riders complained mightily about the rear bench seat that barely supported their shoulders and offered no rest for heads.

Praise: The Yukon is a civilian tank. It rolls over everything, especially when equipped with the optional off-road skid plate, as was the test model. It should be on the shopping list of anyone looking for a tough, high-riding, four-wheel-drive truck.

Head-turning quotient: People look up to the Yukon. They have no choice.

Ride, acceleration and handling: Rides like a truck. Moves like a truck. Accelerates like a truck. That is, it moves with more noise than fury from the starting line, which is fair. People need a chance to get the hell out of the way of this thing. The test model was equipped with the standard 5.7-liter V-8.

Mileage: Hah! If we made money as fast as the Yukon drinks gasoline, we'd all be rich! About 15 to the gallon (30-gallon tank, estimated 440-mile range on usable volume of regular unleaded), running mostly highway with one to four occupants and cargo loads ranging from 100 to 600 pounds.

Sound system: Four-speaker, AM/FM stereo radio and cassette by Delco. Rumble boogie, heavy on the bass, not much on taste.

Price note: The Yukon closed the 1993-model year with a retail price of $20,243 and a dealer invoice of $17,713. Expect modest changes in the 1994 model to bring a modest price increase. But, hey, there's ample enough room to bargain here.

Again, compare full-size Yukon/Blazer prices and take the lowest price. Same truck. Different names.

Hometown: The Yukon and Blazer are assembled in Janesville, Wis.

P.S.: Okay, so I *did* say something else about the Blazer. Big whoop.

ISUZU Rodeo

The Isuzu Rodeo is an aggressive wannabe — a wannabe Jeep Grand Cherokee, a wannabe Ford Explorer, a wannabe taken seriously in the U.S. light-truck market.

I take it seriously.

Honda Motor Co. Ltd. apparently takes it seriously, too.

Honda will start selling Rodeo-based sport-utility vehicles in 1994.

Hey, why not? The Rodeo is a good suvvie made even better with the reworked, Isuzu-developed, 175-horsepower, 3.2-liter V-6 engine. The thing can run.

And, surely, anyone who's seen a new Rodeo has to give it credit for being a good-looker — well-dressed, and sassy at that.

The Rodeo, especially in two-wheel-drive form, will satisfy most buyers who believe suvvies are tall station wagons with knobby tires. These buyers are immune to the Great American Potency Syndrome (GAPS) — the uncontrollable desire to flex muscles that aren't really there and, even if they were real, could never be used.

GAPS-afflicted buyers, on the other hand, often purchase the most rugged four-wheel drive vehicles, even though they'll seldom take those machines off-road. Theirs is the mentality that's spawned fleets of suburb-

Complaints: Poor instrument panel

Praise: Overall excellent construction. Worth a serious look

Head-turning Quotient: Very attractive

Ride, Acceleration, Handling: Very good

Brakes: Excellent

Suggested Retail Price: $14,249 - $22,679

Mileage: About 16 MPG

U.S. Content: 70%

Isuzu Rodeo

One of the most

attractive suvvies

available.

crawling Range Rovers, complete with brush guards.

The Isuzu Rodeo cleverly fills the gap between the GAPS and the anti-GAPS.

In two-wheel-drive with its standard 2.6-liter, inline four-cylinder engine, the Rodeo is, indeed, nothing more than a tall station wagon meant to look rugged.

In four-wheel drive, with the proper equipment, the Rodeo is capable of running off road. But it falls below the abilities of the Explorer, Grand Cherokee and Range Rover in that regard — which is okay.

The Rodeo is a passionate devotee to the idea that you must fake it 'til you make it. It's fakin' it pretty good, right now. In a few more years, with a bit more sophistication, it'll be makin' it on its own.

Background: American Isuzu Motors recognized that its Trooper, a true suvvie, had a loyal, but limited following. So, the company brought out the Rodeo in 1990 to broaden its sport-utility customer base, to bring in more young people and to take in many of those folks who wanted an "off-road" vehicle that they would never take off road.

The early Rodeos, powered by 3.1-liter V-6 engines made by General Motors, were pleasantly attractive bummers. They made a good first impression that faded quickly. In short, the early Rodeos with their chronically downshifting engines, simply weren't up to task.

Isuzu in 1993 did a major overhaul, bringing in its own 3.2-liter, single overhead-cam, 24-valve V-6. That engine is rated 175-horsepower at 5,200 rpm with a maximum torque of 188 foot-pounds at 4,000 rpm. It's offered as standard equipment in the rather pricey LS Rodeo. This engine can be used with an available five-speed manual or four-speed automatic transmission. Get the automatic.

The base S Rodeo gets the 2.6-liter, inline four-cylinder engine rated 120 horsepower at 4,600 rpm. Maximum torque is 150 foot-pounds at 2,600 rpm. The five-speed manual transmission is standard in this application.

Four-wheel-drive Rodeos use manually operated, two-speed, part-time 4x4-gear transfer cases. The standard automatically locking hubs are engaged whenever the transfer case is shifted into 4WD-Low or 4WD-High.

For 1994, the Rodeo remains pretty much the same as it was in 1993, with the exception of a rear high-mounted stoplight, and guard beams in its four doors to reduce the risk of injury in side-impact crashes.

Standard brakes include power, ventilated front discs/rear drums on the four-cylinder Rodeos, and power four-wheel discs (ventilated front) on the V-6 models. A rear-wheel, anti-lock brake system is standard on all models.

Towing, cargo, seating capacities: The Rodeo can be equipped to carry gross payloads, including passengers, of up to 1,015 lbs. It can be equipped to pull a trailer of up to 2,000 lbs. The Rodeo carries five passengers.

Complaints: The instrument panel remains a bit of an ergonomic disaster area. Gauge and control presentation sub-par, especially when compared with the Grand Cherokee and Explorer.

Also, the "power-drive" selector in the four-speed automatic Rodeos strikes me as worthless. The selector is supposed to help bring about smoother up-shifts. I didn't notice any discernible improvement in the Rodeo's behavior with the selector on.

Praise: Overall excellent construction and general road performance. Value per dollar was once an outstanding plus. That's no longer the case, especially given the competition. But the Rodeo is worth a serious look.

Head-turning quotient: Very attractive, one of the most attractive suvvies available. Pretty, in fact.

Ride, acceleration and handling: Very good ride and acceleration. Good handling. Somewhat trucky, but quite manageable. These comments apply to the V-6 Rodeos, especially the long-tested LS V-6 model. I've been singularly unimpressed with the four-cylinder models.

V-6 acceleration is good. Braking is excellent.

Mileage: In the 1993 LS V-6, about 16 to the gallon (21.9-gallon tank, estimated 335-mile range on usable volume of regular unleaded), running mostly highway with one to five occupants and light cargo.

Sound system: AM/FM stereo radio and cassette with compact disc, installed by Isuzu. Excellent.

Price: The Isuzu Rodeo closed the 1993-model year with retail prices ranging from $14,249 to $22,679. Dealer invoice prices ranged from $12,825 to $19,732. Expect price increases in 1994 with modest equipment changes.

Hometown: How's this for fakin' it until you make it? All auto makers have to brag about something. American Isuzu Motors likes to boast that its Rodeo is the "Best-Selling Import SUV(vie)," even though the thing is made in Lafayette, Ind. by Subaru-Isuzu Automotive Inc.

Complaints: Needs better seats
Praise: Excellent overall construction. Superior drive feel
Ride, Acceleration, Handling: Beats everything in its class
Brakes: Excellent
Suggested Retail Price: $18,990 - $29,471
Mileage: About 16 MPG
U.S. Content: 85%

JEEP Grand Cherokee

The drive to Atlanta was turning into a bore. I wanted a diversion, and found one.

There was a vacant excavation site adjacent to southbound I-85 — the diggings for a road in the making. It was temptation enough, and I yielded. I pulled off the highway, plowed into the dirt and spent some moments there scooting around in the Jeep Grand Cherokee Laredo.

It was the first and only time during the 650-mile run from Washington to Atlanta that the Grand Cherokee was used as its maker intended — in the rough, in the mud. That was fun; but it didn't last.

Across the way, on a shoulder of northbound I-85, a South Carolina state trooper stood outside his car. He was looking in my direction. I parked the Grand Cherokee at a high spot on the excavation site, got out of the vehicle and waved to the trooper. Friendliness is the best defense in such situations.

The trooper appeared to wave back. So, I waved again — sort of like a "see-you-later" wave. I climbed into the Grand Cherokee and returned to the highway.

Then, the doubts began. That trooper, was he waving or beckoning? Paranoia overcame my desire for manageable adventure.

I held fast to the speed limit during the rest of my trip through South Carolina; and I kept an eye on the rear-view mirror until I reached the Georgia line.

Background: The Jeep Grand Cherokee was totally redone for the

Jeep Grand Cherokee

1993-model year, which left little immediate room for improvement in 1994. However, there are some incremental gains: front and rear door beams for side-intrusion protection; available built-in, child-safety seats; new asymmetrical off-road tires; ozone-friendly air conditioner refrigerant; a new name for the base model, now dubbed the "SE."

One change involves an elimination — say "Goodbye" to the Cherokee Grand Wagoneer, which is discontinued for 1994.

All remaining Grand Cherokee models come with a standard driver's air bag (facial type) and standard four-wheel, anti-lock brakes.

The base engine for the Grand Cherokee is a 4-liter, inline six-cylinder hummer, rated 190 horsepower at 4,750 rpm. Maximum torque is 225 foot-pounds at 4,000 rpm. A five-speed manual transmission is standard with this engine. A four-speed automatic is optional.

A 5.2-liter V-8 is optional for 1994 Grand Cherokee models. That engine is rated 220 horsepower at 4,800 rpm with a maximum 285 foot-pounds of torque at 3,600 rpm. It's mated to a standard, four-speed automatic transmission.

There are two- and four-wheel-drive Grand Cherokees. The 4x4 models can be equipped to operate part-time, or automatic full-time four-wheel-drive.

Three Grand Cherokee trim levels are available: the base SE, the mid-line Laredo, and the more-sumptuous-than-necessary Limited.

Standard brakes include front discs/rear drums on the SE and Laredo with anti-lock backup. Four-wheel discs with anti-lock are standard on the Limited.

Towing, cargo, seating capacities: With the 4-liter V-6, the Grand Cherokee can be equipped to pull 2,000 to 5,000 lbs. With the 5.2-liter V-8, it can be outfitted to carry up to 6,500 lbs.

Maximum Grand Cherokee payload is 1,150 lbs., including occupants and onboard cargo in this instance. Cargo volume is 40.1 cubic feet with the rear seat up and 81 cubic feet with the rear seat down.

Complaints: It would be nice if the Grand Cherokee had the Ford Explorer's seats, which are more willing to conform to the imperfections of the human body. Also, I have mixed feelings about Chrysler's decision to keep the full-size spare tire in the Grand Cherokee's cargo area. On the one hand, the tire takes up needed cargo space in this compact sport-utility vehicle. On the other, in the event of a flat, the Grand Cherokee's spare is a lot more accessible than the one on the Explorer, which is mounted to a rear body frame underneath the vehicle.

Praise: Excellent overall construction, superior drive feel (as tight and right as some sports cars), excellent instrument panel layout.

The new Jeep Grand Cherokee is one of the best sport-utility vehicles, or "suvvies," available at any price. Its closest competitor is the Ford Explorer, which has been selling like crazy, even in the depths of recession. Indeed, since its introduction in 1989, the Explorer had been chewing up the landscape around Chrysler Corp.'s Jeeps.

But based on strong consumer response to the first run of redone Grand Cherokees, it seems as if that feast is about to end.

Ride, acceleration and handling: Beats everything in its class. The ride is tight, sure, and free of the bounce that still afflicts the Explorer; and it's bereft of the weightiness that turns a drive in the Isuzu Trooper or Toyota Land Cruiser into manual labor.

Acceleration with the standard inline six-cylinder engine is good. Braking is excellent.

Mileage: About 16 to the gallon, which means the Grand Cherokee Laredo rides like a car, but still drinks like a truck. Fuel capacity is 23 gallons. Estimated range on usable volume of regular unleaded is 360 miles — driver only, mostly highway, light cargo.

Sound system: Base four-speaker, Chrysler-installed AM/FM stereo radio and cassette in the test vehicle. Adequate.

Price: The Jeep Grand Cherokee closed the 1993-model year with prices ranging from $18,990 to $29,471, the highest 1993 price being for the now-defunct Grand Wagoneer. Dealer's invoice prices ranged from $17,296 to $26,549.

The Grand Cherokee Limited, now the highest-price member of the line, finished the 1993-model year with a retail price of $28,670 and a dealer invoice of $25,845. Demand is high for these vehicles. High demand yields at least modestly higher prices in 1994.

Hometown: Detroit. That's right. Detroit. The Grand Cherokee models are made at the all-new Chrysler New Jefferson Assembly Plant *in Detroit.*

JEEP Wrangler Sahara

The rain was turning dust into mud and forming little brown rivers everywhere. The day was funky, to say the least — wet and overcast, somewhere between warm and chilly. Certainly, it would have been nice to stay indoors and maybe finish reading the book on the bedroom shelf, or pay some bills.

But I couldn't resist the temptation of that splendid slopmobile in the driveway, the Jeep Wrangler Sahara. It was painted "low-lustre sage green metallic," which meant it was light green with speckles and that the paint didn't shine, except in the rain. The Wrangler Sahara had an olive-green canopy of cloth and vinyl, with clear vinyl windows on the side doors and rear cover. Jumping into the thing was like jumping into a motorized raincoat.

Luckily, this raincoat didn't leak — much. But the vehicle it covered was noisy as hell with wind and road noise and the hum-growl of its big, inline six-cylinder engine.

Lord! You've gotta feel the pull of a four-liter six inside a body as small as the Wrangler Sahara's; and when you feel it, whoa! You get some idea of what excitement and passion are about.

Rain or no rain, I was hot to trot. I headed toward Virginia's Shenandoah Valley for no particular reason, other than that it seemed a good place to go in a Jeep on a foul-weather day. Early in the journey, when the rain was falling hardest, I abandoned smooth highways in favor of boonie junctions, where dirt and gravel had been whipped into a stony slop. I slipped the Wrangler Sahara's transfer gear into "4H" — four-wheel-drive, high gear — and drove until the hard rain turned to drizzle, until the weather began to clear, until the fun of a messy day disappeared into hazy sunlight.

Background: The Jeep Wrangler is the essence of Chrysler Corp.'s

Concern: You *can't* drive this vehicle like a car

Praise: Splendid — when used as intended

Ride, Acceleration, Handling: Handles like a little truck. 4 cylinder feels underpowered

Brakes: Good

Suggested Retail Price: $10,925 - $13,343

Mileage: About 17 MPG

U.S. Content: 90%

Jeep Wrangler Sahara

A big, powerful

engine within a

little, bull-dog body.

entire Jeep Division, the soul of what four-wheel-drive, off-road, sport-utility vehicles are all about.

What you have in the Jeep Wrangler is a big, powerful engine within a little, bull-dog body that comes with a standard five-speed manual transmission and a transfer case that has four operating ranges — two-wheel drive, four-wheel-drive-high, four-wheel-drive-low, and neutral.

You can go to four-wheel drive in the Jeep Wrangler without getting out of the vehicle and locking the front hubs. In standard form, that's about as convenient as the Jeep Wrangler gets, which is understandable, considering the vehicle's original design intent.

Jeeps first were designed as military vehicles with a primary mission of moving soldiers wherever they had to go over the most awful roads, or over no roads at all. Jeeps didn't come with hard-tops, air conditioners, and super stereos back then; and, in basic Wrangler form, they don't come with that kind of stuff today.

To get the extras, you've got to order up, which means moving to the top of the Wrangler line and ordering something like the tested Sahara, or the Renegade. The other Wranglers include the base S and the slightly-better-than-base SE.

The Sahara and Renegade are thematic Wranglers, which means they come with specific color schemes, appointments and lettering. Soft tops with vinyl, zip-out windows and two partially locking doors are standard on these models, as are two extra passenger seats in the rear. Hard tops with roll-up windows and two fully locking doors are optional, as is the Wrangler's optional, lockable "Add-A-Trunk" in which you can carry some stuff that won't fit inside the vehicle.

If you live in a community of more than 10 people, get the hard-top and Add-A-Trunk. Otherwise, *never* leave anything of value in your Jeep Wrangler.

The current Jeep Wrangler series was introduced in the 1987-model year, and hasn't changed much since then. There aren't many changes for 1994, either, with the exception of an improved inline six-cylinder engine, an optional three-speed automatic transmission in the base Wrangler, environmentally friendly air-conditioner refrigerant and a rear, center high-mounted stop light (to warn bears and mosquitoes, I suppose).

The base Wrangler engine is a 2.5-liter, inline four-cylinder job rated 123 horsepower at 5,250 rpm. Maximum torque is 139 foot-pounds at 3,250 rpm.

Sahara and Renegade Wranglers come with a standard 4-liter, inline six-cylinder engine rated 180 horsepower at 4,750 rpm. Maximum torque is 220 foot-pounds at 4,000 rpm.

All Wranglers are available with an optional three-speed automatic transmission; but it's a noisy, harsh shifter. Get the standard five-speed manual instead.

Seating, towing capacities: The Wrangler S has standard seating for two front occupants. Rear passenger seats are optional on this model. The Wrangler SE, Sahara and Renegade have standard seating for four.

Both the four-cylinder and six-cylinder Wranglers can pull trailers weighing 2,000 pounds; but the six-cylinder Wranglers do a much better job.

Complaint: More a concern than a complaint. Too many people buy Jeep Wranglers with the silly notion that they can drive these vehicles the same way they can drive a sports car. They can't. The Wranglers' short wheel-bases, high centers of gravity, and heavy front ends say that they can't. The owner's manuals say the same thing, as do the WARNING labels on the driver's-side sun visors.

Maybe, the WARNING labels can be made larger or more explicit. Maybe, they can say something like:

"IT'S ABSOLUTELY STUPID AND DANGEROUS TO DRIVE THIS VEHI-CLE THE WAY YOU WOULD DRIVE ANY PASSENGER CAR, ESPECIALLY ANY SPORTS CAR. IT'S DOWNRIGHT ASININE TO DRINK EVEN ONE BEER AND THEN CLIMB BEHIND THE WHEEL OF A WRANGLER. YOU CAN — IF

YOU ARE CARELESS, DRUNK, OR OTHERWISE INCONSIDERATE — FLIP OVER THIS VEHICLE MORE EASILY THAN YOU CAN A REGULAR PASSENGER CAR. FLIP-OVER, ROLL-OVER ACCIDENTS TEND TO BE FATAL. READ THE OWNER'S MANUAL AND DRIVE THIS VEHICLE IN THE MANNER PRESCRIBED."

Praise: The Sahara and all other Jeep Wranglers are splendid sport-utility vehicles when used and driven within the boundaries of their design intent.

Ride, acceleration and handling: Wranglers are little trucks that ride and handle like little trucks. I really don't like the four-cylinder Wranglers. They feel under-powered. The six-cylinder models are better on the highway and damned sure better for hauling stuff.

Braking is good in all models. Standard brakes include power vented front discs / rear drums. A four-wheel, anti-lock system is optional on the Sahara and Renegade.

Mileage: In the tested 1994 Jeep Wrangler Sahara, about 17 miles per gallon (20-gallon tank, estimated 330-mile range on usable volume of regular unleaded), mostly highway and driver only with light cargo.

Sound system: Optional AM / FM stereo radio and cassette with four speakers, including two rear speakers mounted on the Sahara's overhead Sport Bar, Chrysler system. Excellent.

Price Note: Jeep Wrangler prices ranged from $10,925 (Wrangler S 4WD) to $13,343 (Wrangler Base Soft Top 4WD) at the end of the 1993 model year. Dealer invoices were from $10,525 to $12,127. The Sahara package could boost the price of the Wrangler Base Soft Top by as much as $3,208. The Renegade package could push up the price by as much as $5,000. The Wrangler's are high-demand vehicles. Prices in 1994 are more likely to go up than down.

Hometown: The Jeep Wranglers are assembled in Toledo, Ohio.

Epilog

DETROIT SUNSET

The sky

Shot

The Sun,

Which began to bleed,

And sink

Until it fell behind

The clouds

And died

Somewhere near

Interstate 80

Heading west

Toward Detroit.

— Mary Anne Reed-Brown

P.S. The sun rose again. Detroit lives.

— Warren Brown